Leadership in early childhood

Second edition

Leadership in early childhood

The pathway to professionalism

Second edition

Jillian Rodd

OPEN UNIVERSITY PRESS
Buckingham

Open University Press
Celtic Court
22 Ballmoor
Buckingham
MK18 1XW

email: enquiries@openup.co.uk
world wide web: http://www.openup.co.uk

First published 1994

First published in this second edition 1998

A catalogue record of this book is available from the British Library

ISBN 0 335 20281 0

Printed and bound in Singapore

Contents

Preface

The continuing interest in the issue of leadership in early childhood has encouraged the preparation of this second edition. The
contents of the book have been revised and updated in the light
of recent research, literature and specific comments and feedback
from students, colleagues and reviewers. However, the basic
purpose of the book remains the same, that is to give current and
intending practitioners a better understanding of the nature of
leadership in the early childhood profession and its effect on the
professionalisation of the field. It explores who is or can become
a leader and why early childhood leaders are in a special position
to set standards and expectations for those concerned with the
development of children and the well-being of families. In developing a typology of effective leaders in early childhood settings,
the personal and professional characteristics, skills and responsibilities which are associated with effective leadership in practice
are examined.

The contents of the book reflect the areas of leadership and
associated skills which are considered to be essential for effective
leadership in the early childhood field. The second edition incorporates new material on women as leaders, a typology of an
effective early childhood leader, children's rights and the ethics of
leadership. Research evidence where available has been included.

Chapter 1 defines leadership in early childhood and dis-
tinguishes it from other forms of leadership. The major functions
and styles of leadership, including current research on women as
leaders, are defined and the role of vision is discussed. A typology

of the effective early childhood leader for the new century is described.

Chapter 2 identifies and reviews the communication and interpersonal skills which are the foundations of leadership. Skills necessary for meeting our own needs as well as the needs of others are identified and explained.

Chapter 3 highlights a key issue for early childhood leaders, that of conflict resolution. Conflict is presented as a normal event which can serve a positive purpose if handled effectively. A framework is presented for understanding and managing conflict constructively.

Chapter 4 examines the critical leadership skills of decision making. Effective use of these skills has been recognised as a hallmark of competent leaders in many fields, among them the early childhood field. Different types of decisions and guidelines for decision making are explained as part of the more general issue of problem solving.

Chapter 5 focuses on the advantages of a team approach to leadership in early childhood settings. The stages of team development, team leadership and supervision, as well as strategies for teambuilding are examined. The second-in-charge position is explored in terms of the special opportunity for leadership that it provides.

Chapter 6 pinpoints change and its management as a crucial leadership challenge. An outline is provided on personal and organisational change, sources of resistance to change and strategies both to deal with resistance and to implement change effectively.

Chapter 7 outlines the importance of keeping up with and using research as a means of informed decision making by the leader. Common reasons are discussed as to why research is under-utilised as a source of information by leaders in early childhood along with the value of research findings for early childhood practitioners and their programs. A number of suggestions for encouraging a research culture in the early childhood profession are put forward with action research suggested as an appropriate methodology for improving practice.

Chapter 8 extends leadership in early childhood to consider the practitioners' relationship and interaction with parents and the public. Parents are recognised as partners in the shared endeavour of providing quality care and education which facilitates children's development and well-being. Practitioner leadership responsibilities in the public domain are identified and ways of acting as an advocate for children, families and the profession are explained.

Chapter 9 raises the ethical aspect of leadership and examines the social responsibility of leaders to make decisions based on professional values and ethical principles.

The Epilogue recapitulates the central role that effective leadership will play in the continued professionalisation of the early childhood field. Several suggestions for moving members of the early childhood field along the pathway of professionalisation are put forward.

While leadership is recognised as an increasingly important issue in the continued professionalisation of the field, research into aspects of leadership in early childhood remains scarce and appears to be undertaken by very few academics throughout the world. Therefore, this book is based in the main on personal experience of preparing students and helping early childhood practitioners to understand and manage their leadership roles and responsibilities more effectively. In areas where current research evidence is available, it has been incorporated in order to validate and strengthen the credibility of the argument. The book is written with an appreciation of the range of practical, everyday situations which call for leadership in early childhood contexts.

While there is an abundance of literature on leadership as it pertains to business, industry, human services and education in general, little has been written specifically for the early childhood profession. Kagan (1994:50) queried whether leadership will be regarded as '. . . another of today's passing fads or as a more durable social elixir . . .'. She suggested that despite interest and concern about leadership in early childhood, key questions continue to be asked by members of the field about the nature of leadership. This book attempts to answer some of those questions.

As with the first edition, this second edition addresses the pressing need for material in this area. The definitions, concepts and strategies which are presented are grounded in organisational theory and behaviour and translated to meet the specific demands of early childhood contexts. In compiling the material considered to be essential for leadership in the early childhood field, care has been taken to present the concepts and skills in an applied and practical form reflecting both the field itself and the need to make the material accessible to the novice as well as the seasoned practitioner.

While not wishing to display gender bias, because the

overwhelming majority of early childhood practitioners are women and for the sake of convenience female terminology is generally used when referring to the early childhood practitioner throughout this book.

Acknowledgements

This book is the product of over twenty years of experience in the early childhood field and is a reflection of my opportunities to meet and work with many of the gifted and dedicated women and the few men who make up the field, including family day care providers and coordinators, child-care workers and coordinators, pre-school teachers and directors, government administrators and academic educators. Without their willingness to share their experiences and thoughts with me, I would not have had the impetus to begin this project.

The Lady Gowrie Child Centre in Melbourne played a key role in the opportunities that I had to collect material which is presented in this book.

I wish to thank my friend, Margaret Clyde, for her continued encouragement of my writing, her unstinting support when the going got tough and her generosity in sharing ideas, material and constructive feedback. She is a stimulating and challenging mentor!

Finally, my ideas about leadership have clarified and developed since writing the first edition, particularly through discussions with students, colleagues and friends in the United Kingdom, Australia, United States of America, Canada and Finland. I wish to express my appreciation for the feedback, ideas and inspiration that they have given me.

Introduction

Leadership continues to be regarded as an important professional issue for early childhood practitioners as the new century draws closer. In the quest for increasing quality in service provision for young children and for recognition as professionals with unique expertise who are different yet equal to professionals in other fields, many early childhood professionals consider leadership to be the key element. Pugh (1996:1) identifies a number of features of early childhood practice which may be considered to define essential aspects of leadership by early childhood professionals. Applying Pugh's features to leadership, leadership in early childhood is considered to be about the experiences and environment provided for children, the relationships between adults and adults and children, meeting and protecting the rights of children and adults and working collaboratively, crossing existing artificial boundaries to meet the needs of all concerned with the care and education of young children.

Early childhood usually refers to a developmental period where children are aged from birth to approximately eight years. In many countries, two independent systems operate to provide care and education for young children. Professionals who work in the early childhood field can be employed in a range of programs in one or both of the systems. Child-care professionals are usually restricted to programs which provide home or centre-based care for children from about six weeks of age until they enter primary school. Occasionally child-care professionals work with children up to twelve years of age in out of school hours programs. Early childhood professionals who are trained kindergarten teachers may work in child-care but are qualified to work as teachers in early childhood settings, such as pre-school, kindergarten, nursery school and infant grades in primary schools, with children from three to eight years. At present, these two care and education systems are not integrated. However, the movement towards increasing professionalisation of the early childhood field includes the elimination of the artificial dichotomy between care and education in early childhood.

It is widely acknowledged that the 20th century has seen major changes in the provision and delivery of services for children and families and that those who work in the early childhood area will need to continue to be responsive to accelerating social change in the future. The changing context has precipitated an expansion of roles that early childhood professionals undertake (Stonehouse & Woodrow, 1992), among them the ability to provide sensitive and skilled leadership. In the search to define quality in early childhood, Barbour (1992) argues that early childhood professionals have moved beyond asking questions such as 'Should we . . . ?' to pursue questions of 'How can we . . . ?'. This book addresses the fundamental question of how early childhood professionals provide leadership as a means for ensuring quality services for young children and their families. The leadership style and performance of administrators of early childhood services will impact upon policy and practice and determine the development and implementation of innovative programs (Jorde-Bloom & Sheerer, 1992).

While change has been recognised as a hallmark of the profession for some time, scant attention has been paid to the concept of leadership which is a necessary condition for effective change. What is meant by 'leadership' in the early childhood profession? It is a term which is bandied about in numerous arenas and professions but one which still is rarely discussed in relation to early childhood. The media remind us of the shortcomings of and the need for political leadership. The recession of the 1990s highlighted the need for leadership in business and manufacturing industry. Politicians and current affairs commentators in many countries throughout the world continue to call for better educational leadership. Yet, when the problems associated with rapid change in the early childhood field are examined, little reference is made by early childhood professionals to the absence of leadership within the profession that could facilitate the gradual and systematic implementation of appropriate changes.

A review of the current literature concerning leadership in early childhood reveals that minimal research has been conducted in this area over the past twenty years. It is evident that scant attention continues to be paid by those working in early childhood settings to the new thinking about leadership which is a result of the changing world of leadership in general and the nature of leadership in the early childhood field in particular. This may be attributed, at least in part, to the apparent vagueness and haziness about what is meant by leadership in the early childhood profession. However, the literature base which does exist is sufficient to point to certain key issues. For example, Galinsky (1986), in an analysis of the essential elements of quality child-care, identifies leadership as one of the critical factors. Lewis and others (1992) support this view by highlighting the need for quality teachers who can also provide leadership in the children's services field. Numerous authors, among them, Bredekamp (1992), Peters (1988a) and Vander Ven (1988), argue that a systematic plan, which is related to the stage of professional development of early childhood practitioners, is needed to identify and nurture those who will lead the profession into the next century. Kagan (1994), Rodd (1996) and Waniganayake (1997) stress the dire need for leadership in the early childhood field. Leadership appears to be a phenomenon which has long been considered and continues to be an enigma (Wallace & Wildy, 1995), particularly in early childhood. Further discussion about and definitions of leadership are presented in Chapter 1.

Findings from the available research studies into leadership in early childhood reveal that few early childhood practitioners appear to be comfortable with the leadership, including the managerial and supervisory aspects of working with adults (Vander Ven, 1991; Clyde & Rodd, 1993). The early childhood practitioners from America and Australia appeared to hold a narrow conceptualisation of the professional role as one where the focus was on direct care of and interaction with children. Although 76 per cent of the respondents articulated a need to be 'professional' in their job and 22 per cent entered the field motivated to 'improve the image of the field', they reported not being comfortable with activities that might contribute to the achievement of these goals, such as managing programs, marketing, influencing policy, lobbying, making speeches, fund raising and research. In fact, there was minimal identification with attributes that were related to the instrumental, professional and entrepreneurial dimensions of leadership defined by Vander Ven (1991). The respondents identified more closely with the attributes which Almy (1975) ascribed to early childhood practitioners, for example, patience, warmth, capacity for nuturing and high energy level. Unless there is an identification and recognition of the leadership role and a broader conceptualisation of their professional role and associated skills, members of the early childhood field will not be able to meet the demands for competent program administrators, supervisors, trainers, educators, researchers and advocates. The results of more recent studies conducted in Australia and Britain (Rodd, 1996, 1997a; 1997b) suggest that while the need for increased professionalism and professional self confidence has been understood, early childhood professionals still need to develop a clearly delineated understanding about the breadth and depth of their leadership roles and responsibilities.

The development of leadership skills is a vital and critical challenge for early childhood professionals in Australia and other countries if the provision of socially and culturally responsive services for young children and their families is to be successful in the next century. It will no longer be acceptable (or feasible), as in the past, to rely on colleagues from other professions such as primary teaching, social work or nursing, to provide leadership models and initiatives which can be adapted to the needs and contexts of early childhood services. Nor will it be seen as appropriate for the new professional status which is currently being sought to adopt professionals from outside disciplines and fields as leadership mentors. If the early childhood profession is to achieve professional status equivalent to that of similar or related professions, it will be necessary to nurture and train individuals who will emerge as leaders from within the profession. Empowerment of the early childhood field has to begin with people who feel comfortable in the leadership role at the program level and who will progress to leadership at perhaps government and policy levels. The roots of such empowerment lie in a reconceptualisation of the professional role from the 'grass roots' up.

The restructuring of several training courses and awards throughout Australia and overseas have attempted to break down the artificial dichotomy between care and education (Tayler, 1992; Fleer & Waniganayake, 1994). However, the terminology which is used to denote the leader of a pre-school centre and that which is used to signify the leader of a child-care service has acted to maintain the unproductive division between care and education. Regardless of the form of child-care and early education that parents choose, the needs of the child remain the same. A four year old has the same needs and is entitled to the same quality program whether that child is placed in a long-day care centre, family day care or a pre-school centre. In an attempt to overcome the nomenclature issue, the terms 'early childhood professional' or 'early childhood practitioner' as well as 'the leader' will be used in this book to denote the person who is responsible for the administration of an early childhood service or program. Depending on the area, coordinators of family day care schemes can be responsible for the work of up to a hundred or so family day care providers. The terminology which is necessary to describe both centre-based and home-based care becomes cumbersome in the presentation of some ideas. Therefore, the term 'centre' will be used to include centre-based and home-based care and education programs. With the current move to incorporate pre-school programs within child care services, it is hoped that pre-school teachers will be motivated to perceive any changes as opportunities to expand and modify their considerable expertise in education and to take up positions of leadership in the range of settings which will emerge over the next decade. This will benefit children, parents and early childhood staff.

1

A professional issue

For at least the past two decades, members of the early childhood field have been noted for their reluctance to identify with the concept of leadership as part of their professional role. This is an interesting phenomenon because historically and traditionally early childhood personnel, both as kindergarten or pre-school teachers and more recently as providers of formal child-care, have been trained to demonstrate high levels of autonomy and independence in policy and practical areas. This professional requirement for independent decision making and problem solving skills appears to have arisen out of the physical isolation of early childhood care and education centres (in which the majority of early childhood personnel have been employed) as well as the small number of adults who have been required to operate programs for groups of children in such settings. With the lack of access to immediate support and backup, early childhood personnel have developed autonomous styles and skills for meeting the demands of their situation which, in other working environments, might be called 'leadership skills'. For early childhood practitioners, leadership has been and will continue to be defined in terms of program management (Spodek, Saracho & Peters, 1988; Kagan, 1994). However, recognition of the concept of individual leadership potential, which exists at a personal and centre level, appears not to have been translated into aspirations for more general organisational or professional leadership which could advance the professionalisation of the early childhood field and achieve much needed advances in community credibility and status.

In reviewing the literature on leadership in general, it is evident that the traditional themes and ideas about leadership are not really applicable to early childhood. Kagan (1994) identified the shortcomings of three traditional approaches to understanding leadership: personal characteristics and traits, style, behaviour and strategies and the nature of the task and work culture. She concluded that, for early childhood, these approaches ignored important features of early childhood settings. These are the emergence of multiple, shared and joint leadership conventionally preferred by women, the need for intimacy, flexibility and individualisation of organisational strategies and processes, and an ethos of collaboration and collective success for all. Such features produce a kind of leadership which seems to be especially suited and perhaps even unique to early childhood. A discussion about factors which appear to pertain to women as leaders is presented later in this chapter.

What is leadership?

Looking through the vast collection of literature related to leadership in educational and other fields, it is clear that many concepts and ideas are in fact applicable to leadership in early childhood. In general, leadership is about vision and influence. It is an inevitable process whenever two or more people get together (Bogue, 1985). Leadership can be described as a process by which one person sets certain standards and expectations and influences the actions of others to behave in what is considered a desirable direction. Leaders are people who can influence the behaviour of others for the purpose of achieving a goal. Leaders possess a special set of somewhat elusive qualities and skills which are combined into an ability to get others to do what the leader wants because they want to do it. Leaders are able to balance the concern for work, task, quality and productivity with concern for people, relationships, satisfaction and morale. They combine an orientation towards innovation and change with an interest in continuity and stability for the present. They do this by using personal qualities which command respect and promote feelings of trust and security. They are also responsible for setting and clarifying goals, roles and responsibilities, collecting information and planning, making decisions, and involving members of the

2

group by communicating, encouraging and acknowledging commitment and contribution.

In broad terms, the key elements of effective leadership are the leader's ability to:

- provide vision and communicate it;
- develop a team culture;
- set goals and objectives;
- monitor and communicate achievements; and
- facilitate and encourage the development of individuals.

Current early childhood practitioners generally have considerable skill in setting standards and expectations for the children in their care but appear to have varying degrees of effectiveness in influencing the behaviour of other relevant groups especially parents and other adults. As 'leaders' of young children, they are competent, confident and effective and appear to have considerable skill in getting children to do what they want. However, early childhood professionals appear to be somewhat uncomfortable perceiving themselves as directors, coordinators or leaders of groups of adults, be they staff or parents within a single centre or relevant professionals and other adults in the community.

As part of a project which aims to encourage innovative approaches to leadership training and support for early childhood professionals, Morgan (1997) has attempted to tease out some of the dimensions related to the term 'leadership' when applied to the early childhood context. She suggests that many of the commonly accepted definitions of leadership raise particular issues for the early childhood field. For example, Morgan suggests that when leadership is defined as the position or office of a leader, such as a coordinator or director, certain implications about expectations of leadership follow which can work to exclude other members of staff, such as teachers and child care workers, from access to and responsibility for leadership. When leadership is defined as a capacity, ability or set of competencies to lead, members of the early childhood profession have yet to identify and agree on what capacities, abilities and competencies are related to leadership in early childhood. The aim of this book and the typology of leadership for early childhood professionals which is presented later in this chapter are efforts to respond to this issue. When leadership is defined as the product of the endeavours of an interconnected group of individuals, the possibilty of shared or collaborative leadership is opened up. This type of leadership appears to be attractive to early childhood professionals who perceive diversity as a strength for responding to the constantly changing demands in the early childhood field. When leadership is defined as guidance and direction, it implies the presence of someone to provide such guidance and direction and points back to expectations about leadership which are associated with someone holding a special position or office. The limitations of this deinition have already been discussed. However, many early childhood professionls identify with the concept of guidance because it does not embody the unacceptable conno-tations associated with concepts of power, command and authority. Leadership in the early childhood field appears to be more a result of groups of people who work together to influence and inspire each other rather than the efforts of one single person who focuses on getting the job done (Jorde-Bloom, 1997; Morgan, 1997). It is therefore imperative that all members of the early childhood profession are encouraged to share and discuss their different perspectives on leadership and have access to opportunities for professional training in leadership as well as preparation for its roles and responsibilities.

Unfortunately, the terminology which is used to distinguish between leaders of child-care and pre-school centres has not helped either the early childhood profession or the community to understand the complexities of the diverse leadership roles in the early childhood field (Rodd, 1988). The concept of a 'leader' who influences others in order to administer an efficient, accountable small business or organisation, which includes adult staff and consumers, has yet to be assimilated into the professional role. Early childhood practitioners' perception and comprehension of and confidence in their leadership role with staff, parents and other professionals is not clear or well-developed. This limitation in professional development may explain the leadership difficulties encountered in service provision and the ongoing low credibility and status of early childhood practitioners compared with other services and professions. In addition, narrow definitions of pro-fessional development and career by many early childhood practitioners has left the profession without its own specialised advocates who can guide its members through the political and economic processes which are influential in determining the continuation or otherwise of these services. Many members of the early childhood field appear to be content to confine their work and aspirations to basic or advanced levels of direct care of children rather than to extend their interest and competence to the more indirect care and educational activities related to professional, entrepreneurial and leadership roles and responsibilities with adults.

It is becoming increasingly evident that the future survival and growth of the services provided by specialised early childhood professionals into the next century will depend upon strong, responsible leadership emerging from within the profession. An increasingly sophisticated comprehension is growing by members of the early childhood field about what is involved in leadership, particularly the idea that there are many ways to leadership and different levels at which it can be exercised. As the professionalisation of the early childhood field gathers momentum, people understand that it is not necessary to begin at the top with developing the highly sophisticated leadership skills of policy development and critical decision making in all practitioners. It is more important to identify the roles and responsibilities within the early childhood profession which permit leadership to be exercised at a more grass roots level so that practitioners are able to grasp the complexities of the work that they perform and the opportunities for leadership which exist in their daily working environment. As individual staff members gain confidence in their leadership capability at the centre level, some will become interested in extending their leadership abilities to wider arenas such as active contribution in professional organisations, action research within centres, writing for the profession and becoming politically active on behalf of the field.

How is leadership different from management?

Part of the difficulty in understanding leadership in early childhood stems from a confusion with management. Hayden (1996) offers a helpful explanation of issues relevant to management of early childhood services. However, she does not link management explicitly to leadership. It is important to understand that leadership and management are inherently linked and interwoven. Effective leaders in early childhood need to be aware that their leadership role is more than routine management which focuses on the present and is dominated by issues of continuity and stability (Simons, 1986). The differences between leadership and

5

management are summarised by Hodgkinson (1991) who argues that leadership is:

- an art rather than a science;
- focused on policy rather than execution;
- concerned with values rather than facts;
- to do with generalism rather than specialism;
- the use of broad strategies rather than specific tactics;
- concerned with philosophy rather than action;
- reflective rather than active;
- concerned with human as opposed to material resources; and
- focused on deliberation rather than detail.

The above characteristics point to the fact that successful leaders are more than efficient managers. Rather than focusing on the narrow and specific details of getting through the day and keeping the program running, they tend to spend their time reflecting, deliberating and planning program administration more broadly around values, philosophy, policies and the need to be responsive to change (Jones, 1980). They utilise the staff resources by delegating others to take care of the fine detail required at the management level. Effective administrators incorporate the future-oriented aspect of leadership to program administration where innovation and change are effected through:

- group goal setting, where the wider the participation of staff, the greater the likelihood of commitment by staff to the goals;
- consensus building, where a productive working environment is created by the group taking responsibility for implementing and adhering to decisions;
- personnel development, where staff and parents are helped to grow and develop; and
- program development, where initiative is taken to establish, review, evaluate and modify existing programs.

While it is true that, in order to be an effective leader, one also needs to be an efficient manager, management skills do not equate with leadership skills. A person with highly developed management skills is likely to have structured the administration of the program to give herself adequate time to devote to key leadership functions. A person with poorly developed management skills is unlikely to be sufficiently organised to free up the time needed to focus upon leadership issues. In any case, management skills are necessary but not sufficient for effective leadership.

What is leadership in the early childhood profession?

While the study of management can be found as a compulsory subject in the training of early childhood practitioners throughout the world, the same cannot be said of leadership. The lack of opportunities for leadership training coupled with limited access to experienced role models (Hayden, 1996) and the antithesis many women appear to have towards roles and responsibilities which involve power (Cox, 1996) have acted to impede development of an understanding of leadership as it pertains particularly to early childhood. Although levels of professionalism, accountability and credibility are increasing in the global early childhood profession, the concept of leadership as a means of advancing the field appears not to be as well understood by practitioners. Some early childhood professionals are thinking about leadership in new ways, for example Kagan's (1994) notion of shared leadership and Jorde-Bloom's (1996) notion of participatory management. However, identifying with the concept of and need for leadership by and of women still appears to be problematic for many of those who work in early care and education.

Effective leadership in the early childhood profession is about working towards creating a community and providing a high quality service. This involves:

• influencing the behaviour of others, particularly staff and parents, to contribute to a creative early childhood program;
• administering the program efficiently;
• supervising staff and guiding parents in ways which will enhance their personal growth and professional development and progress; and
• planning for and implementing change in order to improve organisational and professional effectiveness.

There are four basic steps necessary for any leader to make things happen in an organisation:

1 The definition of organisational and individual goals and/or objectives—This will provide a clarification of the service and its purpose, an outline of future directions, a description of procedures and identification of resource requirements and agreed roles and responsibilities for each team member.
2 The setting of individual standards and expectations—Delegated tasks will be outlined in terms of the function of each individual and include measures or standards of performance.

3 The provision of support and feedback—Assistance is provided
   to individual team members to develop their expertise with
   constructive feedback to ensure that performance is maximised.
4 The monitoring and evaluation of outcomes—A process of
   regular review is essential to ensure that the organisation is
   meeting its defined objectives in relation to professional standards and within the specified time frame.

The early childhood leader has a professional responsibility to
attend to child well-being, adult morale and centre goal attainment
which are the concerns of all early childhood programs. Early
childhood leaders should also work in a manner which encompasses three issues defined by Sergiovanni (1990) as essential in
successful leadership.

• Empowerment—where authority and obligation are shared by
  the leader to result in increased responsibility and accountability throughout the group;
• Enablement—where the leader provides means and opportunities for and eliminates obstacles to individual and group
  growth and development; and
• Enhancement—where leader and follower roles are interwoven
  to produce increased commitment and extraordinary performance.

These factors are important in creating and shaping the work
environment for children, parents and staff whereby the leader
sets the tone and psychological climate which is the hallmark of
a quality program.

The uniqueness of each early childhood setting makes it
difficult to specifically define leadership broadly and exclusively.
However, it appears that supporting the development of relationships between the members of early childhood communities and
teamwork appear to be of utmost importance in shaping effective
leadership in early childhood settings (Kagan, 1994; Marsh, 1995;
Walker, 1995; Honig, 1996). Notions of trust, sharing, collaboration
and empowerment also appear to be central to successful leadership (Jorde-Bloom, 1995). The diverse and multi-functional nature
of leadership called for in early childhood settings highlights the
need for leadership to be viewed more appropriately as a continuum which reflects greater or lesser degrees of input from
certain features as demanded by specific situations. Certainly,
leadership in early childhood appears to reflect more gender and
context specific influences than leadership in other fields. A

typology of leadership (Rodd, 1996) is being developed from a series of research studies which it is hoped will unpack the complexity of leadership in early childhood.

Why are early childhood leaders different?

An abundance of literature is available on leadership skills which includes both theory and its practical application. However, little has been written specifically for the early childhood context. Early childhood leaders operate in distinct settings and lead groups of people with specific characteristics. It is important to understand the special circumstances which impact upon leadership in the early childhood field. The available literature evidences a sex role stereotype bias, in that the overwhelming majority of the research has been conducted with men in positions of leadership in groups which usually have a high proportion of men. Therefore, the existing literature may not be appropriate or relevant for early childhood leaders who need to be aware of and respond to the specific characteristics and demands of the field.

A number of limitations in the current literature on leadership can be identified. Until recently, few studies had explored the nature of women in leadership. In an early study, which recognised this omission, Hennig and Jardim (1976) revealed that women behave differently to men in management positions, particularly in relation to three crucial aspects of team leadership: risk taking, tolerance and flexibility. Their findings indicated that, compared to men, women scored lower on all three of these important qualities. However, for nearly three decades, researchers have shown little interest in women in leadership positions generally. More recently, however, interest has been rekindled. Kinney's (1992) work suggested that, in the early childhood field, women differ from men in their leadership style on a number of characteristics. She argues that women perform the same leadership functions as men, for example, empowering, restructuring, teaching, acting as a role model, being open and questioning, but carry these functions out in a facilitating rather than authoritarian style. In other words, women lead in a way to keep the group functioning while men's leadership style seems to be more concerned with power and authority.

The impact of women in leadership positions and the acknowledgment of a 'female ethos' in management (Karpin, 1995:1302) are relatively new phenomena. However, the issues of women as leaders and gender specific approaches to leadership currently are attracting the interest of researchers. Grant (1997:2) claimed that recent studies have indicated that the future of management is 'female' with the more feminine attributes of cooperation, communication, diplomacy and insight preferred over the traditionally male attributes of competition, aggression, hierarchy and logic. Although evidence exists which suggests that the 'glass ceiling' is a very real barrier to women aspiring to and taking up leadership positions (Cox, 1996; Hall, 1996), women are appearing to be more interested in becoming leaders in a range of arenas, among them politics, business and education. Particularly in education, there has been a sizeable increase in women in senior management positions over the past ten years. However, women are still under-represented when compared to men (Gupton & Glick, 1996). Debate continues about whether leadership is a male preserve with women displaying little inclination towards, interest in and/or aptitude for this area or whether the reason women have not taken up their rightful role as leaders in a range of work environments is due to fundamental sex discrimination in hierarchical organisational structures and social justice issues.

The majority of research into women as leaders has been conducted with women in primary and secondary education systems as well as in social service areas and business where the followers are made up of heterogeneous groups of men and women. The major issues which appear to be investigated are whether women leaders shape their behaviour to conform with the traditional male stereotyped model of leadership or whether leaders who are women themselves engage in a gender specific, feminine model of leadership. Yet, in early childhood, where women dominate the field and generally assume the leadership positions which are available, little research has been undertaken. Therefore, current leadership theory, research and practice into gender specific leadership still may not be applicable to early childhood leaders who lead groups which are composed almost entirely of women. However, understanding what is known about the following questions is relevant for leaders in early childhood. Do women lead differently from men? Is there a new leadership paradigm developing based on feminine principles? How does this apply in early childhood?

Looking at the current research findings concerning gender and leadership and women's approaches to leadership, an interesting picture is beginning to emerge   Studies report that women take and are developing a specific leadership repertoire. Although some studies find no gender differences in leadership, many studies report that women engage in a repertoire and style that is different from that of men. Whether this is gender specific or gender related has yet to be established although it is evident that some men who aspire to leadership, particularly in early childhood, are attracted to what is becoming known as a female approach to leadership.

For women who are leaders, and those in early childhood, the picture which is emerging is one of strong leadership within a collaborative framework (Hall, 1996; Kagan, 1994). Women appear to define power differently from men and do not appear to be interested in displays of power (Porter, 1997). Leadership is exercised in a climate of reciprocal relationships where the leader seeks to act with others rather than assert power over others. Brunner (1994) argues that women prefer 'power to' rather than 'power over'. This means that the female approach to power is based on collaboration, inclusion and consensus building. The woman leader tends to see herself as a member of the team. Such leaders are committed to young children and their well being as well as to caring for the staff and others associated with the organisation. With regards to the task, participation and shared decision making is emphasised (Jorde-Bloom, 1995) and leadership becomes a holistic, inclusive and empowering process. Specifically, women leaders engage in behaviours that empower, restructure, teach, provide role models, encourage openness and stimulate questioning (Getskow, 1996). They engage in the commonly accepted leadership behaviours such as:

• vision behaviour—creating a vision and taking appropriate risks to bring about change;
• people behaviour—providing caring and respect for individual differences;
• influence behaviour—acting collaboratively; and
• values behaviour—building trust and openness.

Women leaders appear to utilise communication and interpersonal skills effectively in their interactions with others. Their approach to leadership tends to be on a cooperative and interactive basis rather than a controlling basis. This means that women keep their power base because they are adaptable and not prone to complacency (Porter, 1997). This so-called feminine approach to leadership may be more conducive to the development of early childhood centres as learning organisations. However, because leadership still is very much considered to be a male domain, many women find taking on leadership roles difficult. There are very few role models and mentors for women interested in effective leadership and women appear to have to work harder to prove, both to themselves and the wider community, that they can successfully undertake leadership roles and positions. It is important that women who aspire to leadership do not suffer from unreasonable insecurity about their abilities or create for themselves unreasonable demands for perfectionism. Early childhood organisations need to ensure that mentoring opportunities are available to assist those with leadership aspirations and those already holding leadership responsibilities (Whitebrook & Bellm, 1996; Sull, 1997). Mentoring is one way of nurturing novice early childhood practitioners to perceive themselves as leaders in the profession.

It is not helpful to polarise the argument to try and prove that women are better leaders than men. Rather, it is more helpful to explore what behaviours, attitudes and attributes are more conducive to effective leadership and to the development of learning people and organisations. Leaders should attempt to create a culture where the values and traits which are important to effective leadership are endorsed, be they masculine or feminine stereotyped values and traits. In this way, it will be possible to develop training options which optimise understanding of and engagement in a new leadership paradigm thus avoiding continuing gender stereotyping of approaches to leadership. Effective leaders, both male and female, engage in more challenging, inspiring, enabling, modelling and encouraging practices than their less effective colleagues (Posner & Brodsky, 1994). It is the engagement in effective practice which is important, not the gender stereotype. The relevance of current leadership theory, research and practice may not be applicable to early childhood leaders who lead groups which are composed almost entirely of women.

While the early childhood field in many countries tends to be a female enclave, a world dominated by women, those who are appointed to lead services may have to operate in a wider context which can be largely male dominated, for example, local government councils. Women who are leaders need to understand stereotypical male approaches to management and leadership. This includes developing assertive communication skills and a confident style for appropriate interaction with a range of people. Women who are leaders in early childhood need to acquire a flexible approach to leadership which will enable them to influence and work effectively with women at all levels and men who may be in positions of authority in broader organisational contexts.

The nature of the group which early childhood leaders are employed to supervise is complex. Apart from the children, there is a diverse group of adults which consists of staff who can be young, inexperienced, untrained and who have different agendas and goals for working in early childhood; older, experienced, untrained staff who are able to draw on their own life perspectives and who often are unaware or unaccepting of the value of the professional perspective; trained staff, both young and mature, with different types and levels of qualifications and experience; and parents who usually have different assumptions, expectations and goals from those of staff. It is therefore necessary for the early childhood field to determine its own definition of leadership, the attributes which are related to leadership situations in the field and aspects of the group process which are relevant to frequently occurring situations.

The rationale for the provision of specialist training in leadership knowledge and skills is based on the nature of the group to be led as well as features of early childhood contexts (Jorde-Bloom & Sheerer, 1991). The following issues highlight the need for the preparation of early childhood practitioners to develop their capacity for leadership as an initial step along the pathway to professional effectiveness (Peters, 1988b).

1 There is considerable social complexity of the group where early childhood professionals work directly with parents and staff as well as with children. This requires sophisticated and complex communication skills which can enhance interpersonal relationships and productive social interaction. Team building and conflict resolution skills are essential as well as understanding the specific expectations of, and requirements for, working with children and parents as well as with staff.

2 The work situation is essentially autonomous; early childhood professionals have the greatest responsibility for the greatest number of working hours for the youngest and most vulnerable of children. Because there is substantial freedom from on-the-job supervision, an understanding of leadership and group processes, the possession of a range of organisational and

management skills as well as a high degree of technical expertise is required.

3 Physical isolation from peers and colleagues occurs so that professional judgement about children, families and program management must be exercised in many cases quickly, confidently and independently. Decision making and problem solving skills are essential. In addition, many of the problems encountered in daily practice present an ethical dilemma for practitioners. Familiarity with The Code of Ethics developed by national early childhood professional bodies such as The National Association for the Education of Young Children and The Australian Early Childhood Association (1991) can provide guidelines and direction for many of the difficult decisions that early childhood professionals have to face in their daily work.

4 There is generally a wide range of children and families who attend the centre. Despite the lack of government regulations regarding ongoing training, the diversity of the client group means that leaders must be independently motivated to be well-informed on current research in the area and to upgrade their knowledge and skills in order to make sound professional judgements. Understanding the role of research is essential for innovative decision making by leaders. The ability to make services responsive to current family and community needs by possessing the appropriate knowledge and skills in order to effect change is also important.

5 The stage of personal and professional development at which individuals may be given the opportunity to become a leader varies. Katz (1977; Katz, 1995a) and Vander Ven (1988), (and Piaget (1986) facetiously), have described stages in the professional development of early childhood practitioners and recognise that it is possible for individuals to undertake positions of leadership at a young age or with little experience and while they are still novices, in survival mode.

Are there any essential characteristics of leaders in the early childhood profession?

Although much of the literature disputes the validity of the attribute approach to identifying who will become an effective leader, Bogue (1985) argued that leaders of integrity in education exhibit certain characteristics. In the early childhood field, the term 'education' is defined broadly to encompass care and education. Bogue's characteristics for leaders of integrity illustrate an attitude towards life which appears to have much relevance for leaders in early childhood. These characteristics which are related to the notion of 'The Learning Person' presented in Chapter 2 are as follows.

- Curiosity (an interest in learning);
- Candor (principles and actions being open to public scrutiny and a willingness to speak the truth);
- Courtesy (treating others with respect and dignity);
- Courage (a willingness to risk and dare and a willingness to make mistakes and learn from them); and,
- Compassion (creating trust, empathy, high expectations, hope and inspiration and providing opportunities for individual, group, personal and professional development).

Such characteristics are the foundations for building positive relationships with others and are essential in order to effect leadership. These characteristics are more important for effective leadership than being popular with and liked by members of the group. It is unfortunate that many of those inexperienced in leadership often assume that it is important for leaders to be liked, to know, to be right, to be in control, to be invulnerable and to be rational (Wofford, 1979). However, these assumptions are inaccurate and counter-productive resulting in leaders who feel inadequate to the task. The characteristics suggested by Bogue are more likely to produce confident, trustworthy and courageous leaders who are admired, respected and consequently supported by their followers. Bogue's characteristics can be seen as essential for anyone wishing to work in early childhood services but are pivotal for effective leadership of the diverse groups of parents and staff which characterise the early childhood field.

What are the functions of a leader in the early childhood profession?

Leaders are organisers of time, talent and task (Bogue,1985). In order to provide effective leadership, two elements need to be kept in focus by the leader—task performance and work relationships. These must operate simultaneously to effect efficient progress at work while building morale.

It is the leader's responsibility to ensure that the group moves towards its goal which, in early childhood, is the provision of a high quality program. This element is referred to as task performance and includes any aspect of productivity, getting the job done and anything related to quality of work or performance in pursuit of the aims and goals of the organisation.

At the same time, the leader needs to ensure that the pursuit of task performance is not at the expense of work relationships or, in other words, the quality of life at work. It is also the leader's responsibility to consider the welfare of the other people at work and ensure that group morale is kept high through building and maintaining constructive, interpersonal relationships.

Neugebauer (1985) has differentiated four major leadership typologies which can be found in early childhood settings. Characteristics related to such a typology have been described by Jorde-Bloom, Sheerer & Britz (1991). The styles outlined vary in terms of the degree of emphasis placed upon achieving the task or results and promoting relationships or morale. Neugebauer's styles of leadership are summarised below.

1 The Task Master places heavy emphasis on the task or results and little emphasis on relationships or morale;
2 The Comrade places heavy emphasis on relationships and morale but little emphasis on the task or results;
3 The Motivator places strong emphasis on both the task and relationships; and
4 The Unleader places little emphasis on either results or relationships.

Neugebauer argues that in early childhood settings the situational context of leadership is not as important as the style of leadership. He cites studies of administration which have indicated that the style of leadership in care and early education centres is related to teaching style, the tone of interpersonal relationships and staff involvement in decision making. The democratic Motivator is the style of leadership which is purported to be the key to successful leadership in early childhood settings.

The Motivator style of leadership includes the following characteristics.

- warmth and flexibility;
- sensitivity, creativity and encouragement;
- confidence in the abilities of the staff and their commitment to hard work;

- supportive and non judgemental;
- open, two-way communication channels;
- involvement and participation of staff in goal setting and other important tasks;
- confident decision making and problem solving;
- frequent feedback;
- encouragement of self-evaluation of staff performance; and
- risk taking.

The combination of such characteristics enables the early childhood leader to demonstrate concern for the personal and professional needs of the staff as well as confidence in their ability and responsibility. In this way, both the task (providing a high quality program) and relationships (a harmonious work environment and high morale) can be accomplished.

Neugebauer suggests that of the remaining three leadership styles, only the authoritarian Task Master style is relevant to leadership in early childhood centres. However, while this approach ensures that goals are set and an appropriate program implemented, a number of disadvantages are inherent in this style of leadership. The staff may not agree with the leader's goals and overtly or covertly refuse to implement them in the program. The lack of respect for staff ability to contribute to the decision making can result in frustration and hostility which ultimately will diminish staff motivation to work hard.

Although it is useful to be able to categorise leadership styles, it is not as helpful to evaluate one or another as the 'best' for specific contexts. It must be recognised that leadership styles are not static and despite Neugebauer's claim that situational leadership is less relevant for early childhood centres, there are many situations where a particular leadership style is more effective than another. For example, if a particular centre has experienced a period of chronic change, staff morale might be low. A sensitive leader will emphasise relationships and work on building up group morale and staff self-esteem, that is, utilise the Comrade style, rather than focusing heavily on the job to be done. Another centre might have a leader who was experiencing stress and 'burnout' and withdraws from active participation in the centre, that is, become an Unleader. Staff may then decide to do what they like in the absence of direction from the leader. A new leader coming into this situation may well need to employ a Task Master style to ensure that goals are set and the quality of the service improved. There is even a scenario where the Unleader style could be the most effective style. This might be where the staff are experienced, highly self-motivated, address problems as they arise and have worked well together as a team. Given that the staff are productive and have good working relationships, the leader might decide to decrease her input and let things run by themselves for a while.

In many ways, it is not the style of leadership that the leader believes she is using but how the style is perceived and experienced by the group. If the leader contends that her style is that of the democratic Motivator, but the staff experience the style as that of the Task Master then the leader is really using the authoritarian Task Master style. The differences between the styles can be small and can be a result of how the leader communicates with and relates to the staff. It is the responsibility of leaders to improve their social interaction with staff and parents. The communication style used can determine the tone and quality of interpersonal relationships and social interaction. In Chapter 2, the communication skills which are considered to be most effective for leaders to achieve the task while simultaneously promoting relationships are described.

Who is a leader in the early childhood profession?

The early childhood profession is perhaps unique in terms of the access to designated positions of leadership which can be taken up, if in name only, by practitioners from the earliest stage of entering the field. Qualified kindergarten or pre-school teachers, usually called 'directors' in Australia, have traditionally been appointed as 'the leader' of pre-school centres even though their teacher training has contained little emphasis on knowledge about and skills for working with adults. Their responsibilities have included the provision of an educational curriculum for approximately 50 children of three to five years of age, support to parents and supervision of one untrained assistant. Although largely autonomous, accountability by directors for policy and practice has been to a committee of management and ultimately to the government department which funds the program. The number of traditional sessional pre-schools and therefore directors positions has been declining because, among other reasons, they have not met the demands for service flexibility which are required by the increasing numbers of working parents.

In contrast, the growth of the child-care industry over the past

25 years has been accelerating. Child-care is provided in a variety of settings such as long-day care centres, occasional care centres and in family day care. The leaders of these centres or services usually are called 'coordinators' in Australia and are not required to possess any mandatory levels of qualifications and/or experience. Such child-care centres and services often cater for large numbers of children from birth to five years who spend long hours in the care of staff who may or may not hold relevant qualifications. The issue of the ratio of trained staff to the number of children has been addressed recently in regulations adopted by all states and territories, for example Victoria's Children's Services Centres Regulations (1988). However, it is still possible for untrained individuals to be appointed to leadership positions as coordinators of child-care centres or as administrators of family day care schemes. It is also possible for young, inexperienced recent graduates to be employed as leaders of large child-care centres or services upon graduation from courses which predominantly train professionals to work with children. While these early childhood practitioners are trained to develop programs based on an understanding of the needs of developing children, they have little or no training for working as a leader of a team of adults. It appears that, in Australia as in many other countries, no requirements are made about specific skills, experience or qualifications necessary for the provision of a child-care program for children and the supervision of the group of staff who are employed to operate child-care centres and services.

To date, appointment or promotion to the leadership of an early childhood centre appears to have been based upon the personal qualities and style that an individual brings to a position (Lay-Dopyera & Lay-Dopyera, 1985), exemplary practice with children or longevity at a centre (Jorde-Bloom & Sheerer, 1992). While these appointment practices may have been workable in settings where there were only two adults working together, such as in pre-school centres, the leadership demands of larger child-care and educational centres call for more sophisticated knowledge and skills. Depending on the numbers and ages of the children using a particular service, the numbers of staff employed can be as high as fourteen or more. Quite apart from the demands of providing leadership for families who use early childhood centres, such a large and usually heterogeneous group of staff calls for a more informed and skilled approach to centre and staff management. There are few professions today which have not recognised the advantages in productivity and relationships which result from management and leadership training for suitable staff. The early childhood field is just beginning to recognise that increased professionalism and credibility in the community may be related to trained leadership at a centre level (Jorde-Bloom & Sheerer, 1991; Jorde-Bloom, 1997). However, the trend is still towards people being appointed to positions of leadership on the basis of their personal attributes, exemplary work with children or longevity in the early childhood field rather than on the basis of formal training in program administration, staff management, clinical supervision, group dynamics or specialised expertise in leadership (Jorde-Bloom & Sheerer, 1992). The consistent provision of high quality early childhood services through expert leadership at centre level will lay the foundation for early childhood staff being recognised by the community as having the ability to make leadership contributions to the wider society.

Who can become a leader in the early childhood profession?

One of the difficulties faced by the early childhood profession is identifying those individuals who, with opportunities for personal and professional career development, might emerge as future leaders. Because the early childhood field is dominated by women who, compared to men, place different emphases on family and career at different stages in their lives, it is not easy to assess who will exhibit leadership potential and to what extent this potential will be developed as part of long-term career aspirations. The fact that women who enter the profession are likely to experience training and career interruption due to time taken to establish and nurture a family means that there are structural obstacles to developing and retaining a professional workforce in early childhood. Many women will require access to flexible training programs and a career structure that can cope with them moving in and out of the system according to family commitments. It is obvious that for a large proportion of personnel in this field, a considerable number of years of full and part-time work will be required to accumulate the knowledge, skills and experience which underpin leadership capabilities and which contribute to increased professionalism. All workers who enter the early child-hood field need to be imbued with the belief that personal potential and aspiration for professional growth and leadership can be nurtured throughout their career even if it is disrupted. Ordinary life experience as an adult can provide opportunities to refine the communication and interpersonal skills which are prerequisite for leadership and broaden one's understanding and perspective on life. This can help build a basis from which specific training in leadership can be undertaken. Jorde-Bloom and Sheerer (1992) have demonstrated the power of leadership training for women in the early childhood field in terms of increased feelings of self-efficacy and ability to effect change.

There has been an ongoing debate during the past 40 years about the origins of leadership, that is, can people be trained to be successful leaders or is leadership dependent upon characteristics which are largely inherited? Three main schools of thought have emerged. Firstly, there is the trait approach—do leaders possess certain traits which differentiate them from their followers? Are leaders born or are they made? (Johnson & Johnson, 1996). Secondly, the behavioural approach—do leaders engage in certain behaviour or possess certain styles which influence other people? (George & Cole, 1992). Thirdly, there is the situational approach in which the situation and/or the structure of the task are considered to be influential in determining which style of leadership to use (Storm, 1985).

It is generally recognised that, although certain inherited personal attributes may be associated with leadership, specific leadership skills can be learned. In addition, it seems that leadership potential can emerge at any time during one's life. Therefore, all people are considered to be capable of leading at different times and in different situations. A person can be a leader in relation to a specific group or a specific task. The qualities, characteristics and skills required in a leader appear to be largely determined by the demands of the situation in which the person is to function as a leader. These include the structure of the task and the characteristics of the people in the group. The situational nature of leadership means that there is no exclusive list of personal attributes or styles which are associated with effective leadership. However, a thorough understanding of the needs of the situation which includes the task and the people will enable an effective leader to develop a repertoire of characteristics and skills that is essential for meeting the organisation's goals (Lay-Dopyera & Lay-Dopyera, 1985). Awareness of the needs, capabilities and interests of the group members will assist in the selection of the style of leadership to which the group will be receptive (Jorde-Bloom, Sheerer & Britz, 1991; Kurtz, 1991). This then is the key issue for leaders in early childhood settings—to understand the requirements of the group members and the task in order to match relevant attributes and skills to the situation.

What is the relationship between leadership and professional career development?

It is important to understand the stages of professional and career development for early childhood practitioners. These provide insight into the types of experience gained over time and the limitations which may constrain effective leadership if early childhood practitioners are appointed to positions of leadership before they are, in professional terms, developmentally ready and capable.

Katz (1977; Katz, 1995a) outlines four developmental stages for early childhood professionals. First is the stage of Survival where the main concern literally is surviving and getting through the day in one piece. Second comes the Consolidation period where the practitioner is ready to build on the experience gained in the first stage. The third stage is Renewal where the practitioner is very familiar and competent in the task of direct work with children and she begins to look for new challenges and ways of extending her expertise. Finally, the stage of Maturity is reached where activities and interests are directed towards a meaningful search for professional insight, perspective and realism.

Vander Ven has drawn up a number of formulations which identify stages of personal and professional development in early childhood careers. In an early model, Vander Ven (1988) proposed five stages of professional development which focus upon levels of cognitive understanding regarding the complexity of the early childhood practitioner's roles and the types of responsibilities associated with these roles. The five stages of professionalism include:

- Stage 1—Novice, which describes early childhood staff who function at non-professional levels usually in direct care functions;
- Stage 2—Initial, which describes practitioners in direct care and educational roles under close supervision by a senior staff member;

- Stage 3—Informed, which describes practitioners who have completed formal training and who have made a strong career commitment to the early childhood field;
- Stage 4—Complex, where experienced early childhood professionals have the option of following a career path which focuses on expert direct practice or leadership functions; and
- Stage 5—Influential, where, as a result of long experience in a range of roles and functions, practitioners hold composite, high level, professional leadership roles.

In a later model, Vander Ven (1991) proposed a three stage model regarding stages of career development which is outlined below:

- Stage 1—Direct Care: Novice, describes the usually non-professional (as distinct from unprofessional), affective and professionally immature orientation of young and inexperienced personnel.
- Stage 2—Direct Care: Advanced, describes practitioners who are more able to demonstrate logical and rational behaviour, make choices and predict and explain outcomes of their behaviour. These people have outgrown Katz's stages of Survival and Consolidation and are moving into the Renewal stage.
- Stage 3—Indirect Care, represents a very different role for early childhood practitioners in that they have moved beyond working directly with children and parents and possess the understanding and expertise to take up professional leadership roles and responsibilities.

Leadership potential is considered more likely to emerge in practitioners who are in Katz's Stage 3—Renewal or Vander Ven's Stage 2—Direct Care; Advanced, and be well developed in Katz's Stage 4—Maturity or Vander Ven's Stage 3—Indirect Care.

The continued professionalisation of the early childhood field has been linked to the process of voluntary accreditation of child-care centres which has been introduced in Australia. This process is likely to result in increased leadership responsibility for many early childhood practitioners, with program quality being related to the on-the-job training and supervision of staff who may have had limited experience and formal education and training. This expanded responsibility plus the opportunity to undertake leadership roles from the beginning of one's career in early childhood means that all students and existing staff should be encouraged to acquire an understanding of the essentials of leadership in the early childhood field. The factors outlined above point to the need for leadership skills to be considered as essential to the role of the early childhood practitioner as the fundamental skills of child observation, curriculum design and implementation and program administration.

What is the role of vision in leadership?

Apart from their responsibility to organise time, talent and task, leaders must also demonstrate a capacity to organise ideas and ideals (Bogue, 1985). This aspect of leadership is conducted through the development of a 'vision' which, in the early childhood field, is translated into centre philosophy. The vision is the means by which leaders captivate the imagination of their followers and engage loyalty and support. It is the philosophy which is articulated by the leader and adopted by those adults involved in an early childhood centre which provides the direction for and gives meaning to innovative decisions, the search for new programs, practices, and the policies to improve effectiveness or expand the service. The vision provides direction for and sustains action in the team, can boost morale and self-esteem and act as a buffer against stress during periods of change.

Sergiovanni (1990) has developed a hierarchy of ideas and ideals which is helpful in guiding the leader's organisation of her thinking when addressing the process of developing her vision into a centre philosophy. The entire staff should be included in discussing these ideas and ideals which can contribute to the final centre philosophy statement being perceived as a product of the group process. The philosophy which the leader then uses to guide decision making concerning program policy and practice should include information about:

- The Vision (the leader's hopes and dreams);
- The Covenant or Contract (the leader's, staff members' and parents' shared values and expectations);
- The Mission (the leader's, staff members' and parents' sense of shared purpose);
- The Goals (the strategies which will be utilised to achieve the vision); and
- The Objectives (the tactic and tasks which are appropriate to accomplish the goals).

The vision should be clear and simple, based on underlying professional values, making priorities explicit and indicating expectations about staff participation. A breadth of experience is likely to benefit the development and communication of vision by a leader (Carnall, 1995). Therefore, those early childhood practitioners who bring wide experience and a depth of knowledge will have greater resources to draw on for creating a vision which will inspire the support of the staff.

A typology of leadership for early childhood professionals

From the literature available about leadership in early childhood, it is clear that leadership is an elusive phenomenon (Jorde-Bloom, 1997). While the essential characteristics, skills, functions and responsibilities of leaders, their inter-relationships and the relationship of such factors to stages of professional development are beginning to be unravelled, leadership is essentially a holistic concept in which the whole is more than the sum of the pieces. However, because leadership is a complex construct and sometimes difficult to identify in early childhood settings, a typology of leadership for early childhood professionals may help simplify some of the factors which underpin effective leadership in early childhood settings.

A typology is a means of or framework for classifying selected factors or features. It can be used as a summary or protocol for understanding the structure of a phenomenon. While it can be argued that a typology oversimplifies what may be a very complex concept, it can be helpful for understanding essential component parts, especially where it is believed that certain component parts may be acquired through training. In relation to leadership, a number of inventories, profiles or typologies have been developed which attempt to describe leadership (Jorde-Bloom, 1997). Many of these focus on different conceptions of leadership but few have attempted to relate such profiles to a specific context. It is recognised that the context of leadership, including the nature of the group and the organisational setting, is a determining factor in effective leadership.

The following typology of leadership has been and continues to be developed from research undertaken with early childhood professionals in Britain (Rodd, 1997b) and Australia (Rodd, 1996). Therefore, it is applicable specifically to early childhood practitioners and settings. However, because understanding about what is effective leadership in early childhood continues to grow from research and debate, the typology is and will be subject to development and revision. It should not be considered to be the ultimate definition and analysis of leadership in early childhood. In addition, it is important to recognise that, although effective leadership is essential to improved quality, leaders cannot always achieve the results that they and the team want and the desired results are seldom attributable to one person alone (Jorde-Bloom, 1997). As discussed earlier, leadership in early childhood tends to be a collaborative and shared endeavour.

The typology described in Table 1 is a modified version of an earlier attempt to identify the personal characteristics, professional skills and roles and responsibilities (Rodd, 1996) which are considered to be pertinent to effective leadership in early childhood. One advantage of such a typology is that aspiring and actual leaders are alerted to significant features of effective leadership, thus avoiding a trial and error approach to learning how to be an effective leader. Given that few early childhood professionals have access to leadership training before taking up leadership responsibilities or while in position, the typology may be an effective instrument for signalling important features, developing understanding of what constitutes leadership in early childhood and for enhancing self perception as a leader.

Three different aspects which were identified from survey and interview information provided by early childhood professionals in Australia and Britain have been included in the typology. The groupings of personal characteristics reflect understanding at different stages of professional development. The grouping which describes a set of nurturing characteristics as essential for leadership tended to be identified by those with under three years of experience in early childhood, that is the novices in the profession. For those with longer experience and in leadership positions, such characteristics were perceived as 'givens', that is, all people working with young children and their families would be expected to display such characteristics. Being nurturing is considered to be a necessary but not sufficient characteristic of a leader. However, a nurturing approach to staff and adults associated with the centre was considered to be important in an early childhood leader's general approach. The grouping of personal characteristics which reflect the rational, analytic use of a knowledge base tended to be identified by those with between three and ten years

Table 1 Typology of an early childhood leader

Personal characteristics	Professional skills	Roles and responsibilities
Kind, warm, friendly Nurturant, sympathetic Patient	Technical competence as an early childhood professional to act as a model, guide and mentor	To deliver and be accountable for a quality service To develop and articulate a philosophy, values and vision
Self aware Knowledgeable	General administration	To engage in a collaborative and partnership approach to leadership
Rational, logical, analytical	Financial management	To engage in ongoing professional development and to encourage it in all staff
Professional, professionally confident Visionary Mentor and guide, empowering Assertive, proactive Goal oriented	Effective communication Human resource management	To be sensitive and responsive to the need for change and manage change effectively To act as an advocate for children, parents, staff, the profession and general community

experience, those who were more informed about the complexity of the early childhood profession. Many of the respondents in this group were in fact designated leaders who were very concerned about quality improvement in their own centre. The last grouping of personal characteristics, where vision, professional confidence and empowerment were perceived to be essential for effective leadership, reflected the knowledge and experience of those who had previous leadership experience and training and who took a broader perspective on leadership. These respondents were at more advanced stages of professional development and they displayed an understanding of the complexity of their roles and responsibilities within the centre but also within the wider community.

In relation to professional skills, five major generic areas were identified with none taking priority over the others. The acquisition and display of technical competence were perceived as basic but essential because these were considered to be the vehicles of empowerment for staff as well as the organisation. General administrative ability was considered to be crucial, as was financial management because the viability and smooth operation of the centre were believed to hinge on these two functions. However, it was acknowledged that it was easy to be dominated by these two areas and to accept that effective leadership was simply a result of successful management of centre operations and the budget. Effective leadership in early childhood involved two other key skills from which power and influence in the centre were derived. Effective communication, the ability to 'synthesise complex information and communicate that information cogently and succinctly to a variety of different audiences' (Jorde-Bloom, 1997:13) was regarded to be a hallmark of an effective leader. In addition, human resource management, that is, effective utilisation of the talents, skills, interests and abilities of the group by motivating, inspiring and empowering group members to pursue common goals, illustrated the more feminine approach to leadership by early childhood professionals. The multi-faceted nature of leadership is evident in the generic skills included in the typology.

While the roles and responsibilities of leaders in early childhood centres may vary considerably in relation to specific settings, the respondents identified what can be regarded as a set of generic roles and responsibilities for leaders. Again, no one role or responsibility was considered to take priority. Recognition of the inter-relatedness of roles and responsibilities at the broader level characterised leadership. The delivery of a quality service was perceived as an obvious broad responsibility. The responsibilities for developing and articulating a vision and to engage in a collaborative and partnership style of leadership were considered to be the means for achieving this broad responsibility. In addition, encouraging all staff and engaging oneself in ongoing professional development was thought to be part of the empowerment process. Responsiveness to the need for change was considered to be a means for not only ensuring the survival of early childhood services but for the pursuit of quality. Finally, advocacy was recognised as a responsibility that leaders needed to fulfil but it was thought that this would increase and improve as leaders became more self assured and confident overall.

The typology has attempted to build a picture of leadership made up of characteristics, skills, roles and responsibilities which are generic for early childhood leaders. It is important for members of the profession to decide whether these are indeed requisite features for leaders. When assessing personal leadership potential or that of others, it may be helpful to check which of these features are either emerging or developed and whether or not specific features can be learned. Where features can be learned, it is important for individuals to gain access to professional training or development opportunities to practise, refine and extend them (Thorner, 1997). In many ways, leadership is similar to the concept of quality. Our definition and understanding changes as we learn more about the needs of those associated with early childhood centres. For all early childhood professionals, leadership is about improving those skills which are considered to be related to quality in the profession.

Why does leadership work in some situations and not others?

Sometimes a leader operates successfully in one centre but experiences difficulties in another. There are a number of reasons which explain why this occurs. One of these is that the cultures of the group and the leader do not match or fit. For example, the psychological climate of the group may be focused upon people and their individual needs whereas the leader's style might be task-oriented emphasising organisational needs. Another reason is incompatibility between the leader and significant members of the group. For example, the leader and the second-in-charge or the president of the committee of management might espouse different values and consequently have conflicting goals for the centre. A third instance is where there is a need for task-specific leadership. In this case, there is a mismatch between the nature of the task and leadership style. For example, a task which has to be completed in a specific format and has a specific timeline, such as fee subsidies or funding submissions, requires task-oriented, goal-specific and goal-directed leadership. Other tasks such as program planning can be completed in a number of different ways and therefore left to the professional discretion of the staff member.

In summary, to provide effective leadership in early childhood centres, the leader has to articulate a clear vision of the future and a general plan of action for getting there. She needs to be capable of maintaining a balance between getting the job done and meeting people's needs. Getting the job done involves providing vision by clarifying goals, aims, objectives, roles and responsibilities; gathering relevant information from the staff and parents; summarising, integrating and developing ideas as a way of building a philosophy to guide the group in achieving its goals; and monitoring the group's progress towards the goals through constant evaluation. Meeting people's needs involves clarifying the group goals to help people understand the purpose of the group and to help gain commitment; providing guidelines to help people know what is expected of them in group interaction; providing a sense of inclusion or belonging and acceptance in order to draw on the full resources of the group; keeping channels of communication open and creating a warm and friendly atmosphere in the centre where group members are valued through encouragement and recognition. Motivation, commitment and contribution are stimulated in all adults concerned with the centre when the above issues are addressed by the leader.

2

Communication and interpersonal skills

Human beings are social beings and as such have a need to belong, to find a place in the group (Adler, 1958). People, both adults and children, are motivated to behave in ways which help them achieve a sense of significance in the groups in which they live. When people believe that they belong, they also feel connected, capable and competent, willing to contribute to meet the needs of the group. Alfred Adler's theory of Individual Psychology provides a useful framework for understanding the basis of human behaviour. The values and interpersonal techniques described by Adler, Dreikurs and other authors have been considered appropriate for and relevant to early childhood programs and practices (Harrison, 1991). However, leadership also plays an important role in determining and understanding human behaviour in groups (Robbins, 1996). This is because it is the leader who determines the psychological climate of the group and motivates individual members' level of performance in the achievement of the group's goals.

Successful leadership in the early childhood field is a matter of communication more than anything else. While many of the theoretical explanations of leadership have attempted to identify what makes an effective leader, most studies have dealt with leadership in business organisations or educational institutions (Maxcy, 1991). With few exceptions, such as Jorde-Bloom and Sheerer (1992), Kinney (1992) and Neugebauer (1985), little significant work has been undertaken on what contributes to effective leadership in the early childhood field.

Early childhood services are specifically 'people' services where communication and interpersonal relationships are the foundations or the building blocks on which other activities, such as developmental programs and curricula, are based (Rodd, 1989). Positive human relationships between adults and children and between adults themselves are regarded as both the building blocks of the service and an outcome of the service. Better relationships are considered to develop out of feelings of safety, security and trust and are characterised by openness and sharing between people. These qualities are created and maintained by the type of interaction which takes place between people (Johnson, 1996). Leadership in the early childhood field is more than the style used, the personal attributes and psychological characteristics of the individual in charge, the conditions where and the settings in which leadership emerges. It is about how communication skills, the early childhood professional's tools of trade, are used as a means of building more satisfying relationships. Such relationships contribute to enhanced development and learning by children, parents and the staff who are part of the service (Rodd, 1987). Given that it is the responsibility of the leader of an early childhood service to ensure that the service meets a diversity of needs and expectations in a range of consumers, it is essential that the leader understand the importance of her self-presentation and performance in the area of communication and its relationship to leadership.

Because every leader plays a unique part in setting the psychological climate of the organisation (George & Cole, 1992), the leader needs to demonstrate a certain level of self-awareness and understanding in order to be able to influence others, both children and adults, through interpersonal communication. To gain the basic trust and confidence of others which are fundamental for the operation of a quality early childhood service, the leader needs to convey a specific set of attitudes and beliefs to others. In other words, the leader must create an image or profile which will be genuine, attractive and inspirational to the people that she works with. The following attributes are regarded as essential for a leader of an early childhood service.

First, a leader must convey confidence in herself and the early childhood profession. The personal style of an early childhood leader can influence how she is perceived by children, adults, staff and other professionals which in turn can determine how the profession is perceived by the overall community. A leader who does not believe in her own ability to do the job well, perhaps as a result of limited self-understanding of values, attitudes, strengths, weaknesses, roles, responsibilities and goals or a lack of valuing of importance of the profession, will convey these attitudes and beliefs in subtle, non-verbal ways and in more overt ways to those people she interacts with. On the other hand, a confident and enthusiastic leader who communicates through beliefs, actions and words that she has a strong sense of self, and is committed to making an impact on the lives of the children and adults she interacts with, will attract followers who are willing to be guided in the direction taken by the leader.

For parents in particular, it is important that the early childhood leader convey confidence and a genuine acknowledgement of the importance of the job. Parents place their most important extensions of self, that is, their children, in the care of early childhood practitioners. The anxiety and mixed feelings reported by many parents can be exacerbated or diminished by the personal presentation of the leader. A confident leader has the potential to reassure parents that she has the welfare of the child in mind and will ensure that the child spends a happy and productive day.

A confident leader can assist staff through displays of positive attitudes about their contribution to children's and parents' growth and development and model positive ways of coping with the daily demands of working with young children, relating to parents who may be vulnerable, stressed or have unrealistic expectations, and of simply getting through the day in this people-intensive working environment.

Secondly, a leader who is able to inspire the confidence and support of children, parents and staff will have a well-developed understanding of the positive aspects of herself and will have taken the time to get to know herself. A successful leader needs to have a high level of proficiency in a range of skills, for example, motivating, delegating, financial management, planning, and curriculum design but will also accept that personal and professional growth takes time and is, in part, a result of experience. Such a leader will be able to make a realistic self-assessment of assets and limitations and will not understate or overstate what she brings to the early childhood setting. Nor will such a leader be harshly or overly critical of her shortcomings but will accept that it takes time to develop the sophisticated and complex skills that are needed for working with and leading other people.

Thirdly, an effective leader needs to have a positive attitude to new experiences. The history of early childhood is a history of change with a tradition of action, with some daring and risk taking and considerable persistency which has been produced by a combination of societal, cultural, political and economic forces. These forces necessitate leadership activities in the macro contexts of social development and change, the meso contexts of groups and organisations and the micro context of individual relationships (Maxcy, 1991). Given that change has been part of the fabric of the early childhood profession, leaders in the field need to develop a positive attitude to new experiences and change in general.

Dunphy (1986) describes individuals who perceive change as a challenge and therefore possess the power to create change as 'The Learning Person'. Such a person possesses characteristics similar to the ones described by Bogue (1985) which are outlined in Chapter 1. The core features of a Learning Person are robust self-esteem, openness of communication and a wide behavioural repertoire which permit confidence rather than crisis in the face of challenge and a flexible problem solving approach in response to new experiences. At the other end of the scale, Dunphy (1986) describes the individual who is not open to new experiences and who is resistant to change as 'The Self-Defeating Person'. This type of person exhibits either a low or inflated self-esteem, defensive communication and a routinised, inflexible behavioural repertoire which fosters an unwillingness to risk new experiences and a perception of change as threatening. A positive attitude to new experiences is an integral part of the process of the professional development and transformation of early childhood practitioners into leaders.

Fourthly, an effective leader has a positive attitude to relationships with others and considers that the quality of relationships in the workplace is as important as the task-related aspect of goal achievement and will place value upon activities that assist her with really getting to know children, parents and staff. Such a leader is interested in the effects of her own behaviour upon others, uses feedback to modify her own behaviour and is willing to try different ways of relating to other people. The leader can see the benefits of building and maintaining satisfying and harmonious relationships as a way of meeting children's and adults' need to belong and feel significant in the group and as a way of providing mutual support between the providers and consumers of early childhood services.

Developing positive attitudes to relationships with others is essential for leaders in the early childhood profession because children's optimum development and learning is dependent upon quality interpersonal relationships (Feeney, Christensen & Moravcik, 1996), as is the quality of partnership which will develop between staff and parents. In addition, staff morale, commitment and performance levels are affected by attitudes to and expectations about relationships in the workplace. Positive attitudes to relationships can influence staff to interact with each other (and the leader herself) in a caring and constructive manner. The extent to which children, parents and staff feel trusted, accepted and respected by the leader will determine the quality of communication and interaction.

Finally, an effective leader has positive interaction with others. Even though individuals may have the best of intentions about interacting with others positively in the workplace, disagreement, dispute and conflict are inevitable. This is particularly likely in work contexts where individual and personal value systems can influence and determine professional policy and practice (Brill, 1995). The early childhood field is one in which individuals (parents and staff, trained and untrained, mature and young, experienced and inexperienced) bring their own subjective, highly personalised, socially and culturally determined beliefs and values about child rearing, child-care and early education. An effective leader will understand the destructive impact of inappropriate, negative interaction styles on levels of trust, feelings of security and safety and on performance, and will actively model and promote mutually respectful, cooperative and collaborative interactions with others as a means of enhancing the general self-esteem and goal achievement of the group.

Communication skills for effective leadership in early childhood settings

Many books are available for professionals and others interested which outline and explain communication skills that have been found to be helpful in personal and professional relationships. Kotzman (1989) has drawn on her own experience as a kindergarten teacher and psychologist in her book which focuses on communication skills for early childhood practitioners. Johnson (1996) and Bolton (1986), among others, have written readable and practical guides to communication skills and interpersonal relationships. The focus of this chapter is to link specific communication skills in a way that recognises the context in which early childhood leaders work and which does not relegate personal communication to the merely mechanical sending and receiving of messages.

In analysing the responsibilities of leaders in early childhood settings, there appear to be two major areas of responsibility which need to be balanced in order to survive at a personal level and effectively achieve the goals of the service. Firstly, as an early childhood professional, it is important to meet the needs of other people. There are specific communication skills which are helpful in meeting this responsibility. Secondly, it is essential that skills for meeting our own needs in the work context are developed. While there is some overlap between the two sets of skills, they can essentially be divided into two groups set out below.

Skills for meeting others' needs	*Skills for meeting our own needs*
• Sending accurate and unambiguous messages	• Appropriate self-assertion
• Overcoming physical and psychological barriers	• 'I' messages for 'owning' statements
• Listening for understanding	• Conflict management
• Appropriate responding	• Delegation
• Managing feelings	• Time management
	• Stress management

Many early childhood practitioners will claim that they have no problem with their communication skills, no difficulties in understanding others and being understood themselves. While this may be true at one level, there is always room to improve skill in this area. It is not sufficient for early childhood leaders to communicate at the basic 'get-the-message-across' level. More sophisticated and complex skills are required to deal with the variety of situations which present themselves when the job involves working with people. It would not be acceptable for a cabinet-maker to build a fine piece of furniture with a second-rate, blunt and rusty saw. In the same way, it is not acceptable for early childhood professionals to consider fulfilling their roles and responsibilities with second-rate, unrefined communication skills.

Because the early childhood leader's primary responsibility is to meet the needs of others, such as children, parents and staff, the skills for meeting others' needs will be described first.

Skills for meeting others' needs

Effective communication in the early childhood context is dependent in many ways upon the leader's sensitivity to other people's need to feel understood. It is the leader's responsibility to create an emotional climate from which self-disclosure, empathy and honesty will emerge and foster the perception of 'being understood'. The skills that the leader employs to communicate with others on a day-to-day basis contribute to that process.

Sending accurate and unambiguous messages

Early childhood services are 'people' services where the business of the day is, providing quality care and education programs for young children, understanding parents' needs and expectations, supporting them in their parenting role and utilising available staff resources effectively. Communication plays an important role in all of this. While early childhood practitioners who are trained in child development possess a good understanding of young children's language and communication abilities and limitations and attempt to match the style and complexity of messages to children's developmental capabilities, this sensitivity may not extend to communication with adults. Given that it is the leader's responsibility to disseminate large amounts of information at different levels within the early childhood setting, it is important to consider the extent to which clear, accurate and unambiguous messages are constructed for the intended receiver.

Such messages are constructed from a consideration of the characteristics of the intended receiver, the need to have the message understood in the way that it was intended and an awareness of points of potential breakdown. Because verbal messages are usually sent only once and compete with all sorts of distractions, it is essential that care be taken with the construction of these messages and that the sender not assume that the message was understood as it was intended. The communication styles used by sensitive early childhood practitioners are different for babies, toddlers and four year old children. Similarly, when constructing a message account should be taken of the needs of parents versus staff, that some people are from non-English speaking backgrounds, that staff includes trained and untrained, experienced and inexperienced people, as well as the importance of the message. Because people tend to hear what they want to hear it is important to check the recipient's understanding of the message. Early childhood professionals do this with children and need to ensure that they use this skill in their communication with adults.

Overcoming barriers to communication

Since anything that competes for our attention can be a barrier to effective communication, clearly, early childhood centres are not conducive to effective communication. The physical setting with staff isolated in separate rooms, the staff roster system, the noise that young children make, the constant ringing of the telephone, the interruptions by parents who want staff attention immediately and the primary child supervisory responsibility of the staff, all militate against effective communication and increase the possibility of communication breakdown. Although not all communication exchanges require high levels of skill, certain situations, such as dealing with a parent complaint, providing feedback to staff and obtaining information about the progress of a certain child, require discreet and tactful handling. The effective leader is aware of the range of barriers to communication within the centre and considers ways in which their impact can be eliminated or minimised. Barriers to communication which exist in physical settings can be manipulated and used by those who wish to sabotage communication efforts. For example, people may be using barriers to prevent effective communication taking place when they deliver an important message to a listener who is occupied with a group of children in a noisy toddler room, when they call a message out as the listener passes by the office or at the same time that they are involved in a telephone call or when they give unnecessary attention to distractors and interruptions.

The physical barriers in an early childhood centre can be handled relatively easily when compared with the psychological barriers to effective communication. These consist of the subjective attitudes, values, beliefs, stereotypes and prejudices that all of us bring to a communication exchange. It is interesting to note that many of our subjective and enduring attitudes which we use to interpret the messages we receive are formed by the age of five. This is why it is important for early childhood practitioners to be aware of the sub-context of communication with children and adults. While on the surface it may appear that a particular message is being conveyed, the existence of underlying value-laden messages can influence how it is understood by the receiver.

Leaders in early childhood services need to be aware of their own and their staff members' values, attitudes, prejudices and stereotypes which may influence how they understand and meet other people's needs. What we hear other people saying can be coloured by our own preconceived judgements. Take the example of a teenage mother who comes to discuss the behaviour problems that she is experiencing with her four year old boy. Certain value judgements may spring to mind immediately, such as poor, uneducated, inexperienced, neglectful, incompetent, irresponsible, immoral and so on. In fact, none of these may apply to this person. However, if such value judgements dominate the way in which the leader or the staff perceive the mother, they will act as barriers to communication and influence how well mother's need to be understood and supported is met. Sensitive leaders do not underestimate the power of psychological barriers to interpersonal interactions.

Listening for understanding

Johnson (1996) argues that the most effective communicators are those who are able to put aside their own egocentric preoccupation with speaking and instead direct their attention and energy to listening for the meaning behind what the speaker is saying. This type of listening is different from simply hearing the words. While there are often many distracting noises in the background such as cars passing by, doors banging or the radio next door, we do not specifically listen to them unless they are meaningful in some way. When we listen, especially in a professional capacity, we are trying to meet others' need to be understood. Therefore, it requires that an effort be made to comprehend and use all of the available information to understand the meaning of the message as it was intended. This kind of listening is referred to as 'Active Listening' or 'Reflective Listening' in the literature on communication.

To summarise what is involved in listening for understanding, the listener first ensures that she has the appropriate time and space to devote to the speaker. If time is likely to be insufficient to meet the speaker's needs, the listener needs to convey interest in the speaker's issue and negotiate a more appropriate time to devote to the speaker. If the time is suitable, the listener needs to eliminate or minimise potential barriers to communication, such as redirecting telephone calls, preventing interruptions and sitting in positions which communicate positions of equality rather than power. Secondly, the listener deliberately focuses attention on the speaker by using appropriate eye contact, body posture and non-verbal communication to indicate that she is interested in and following the speaker's issue. Thirdly, the listener gathers information from three sources from the speaker—the content, that is, the actual words heard, the speaker's body language or non-verbal communication (which is a more reliable guide to the accuracy and importance of the verbal content) and the paralinguistics, that is, how the speaker says the words (tone of voice, emphases, breathiness, fast or slow delivery). Fourthly, the listener uses all of these sources of information to interpret the speaker's message and reflects and clarifies her understanding in a short recapitulation of the essence of the speaker's message. Finally, the listener modifies her understanding of the speaker's intended message in the light of the speaker's response to the listener's clarification. This process communicates interest, empathy and respect in meeting the speaker's need to be understood and encourages further communication and interaction.

Appropriate responding

In the communication process, listening is the most important skill which needs to be developed in most people, children and adults. However, communication is a two-way process and the way in which early childhood professionals respond to children, parents and staff affects the quality of the interaction.

Carl Rogers (1961) delineated five response styles which accounted for approximately 80 per cent of the verbal communication engaged in by professionals in human service occupations. The other 20 per cent consists of the unintelligible grunts, groans and acquiescent noises that people scatter throughout their conversations. He argued that all people develop preferred response styles which tend to be produced automatically in the short space in which a timely response is expected to ensure the flow of human communication. Rogers believed that the use of one response style for 25 per cent or more resulted in the speaker being stereotyped by the listener as 'always' responding in that way. The effect of this stereotype is considered to diminish people's perception of being understood, blocking further communication and decreasing the possibility of the listener meeting others' needs.

The five response types Rogers described are:

- Advising and Evaluating—typical responses are 'What you should do now is . . .' or 'If I were in your shoes, I'd . . .';
- Interpreting and Analysing—responses would be 'The problem you really have here is . . .' or 'You've missed the point! The real issue is . . .';
- Supporting and Placating—the aim is to diminish emotions in responses such as 'Don't worry, they all go through that stage!' or 'Forget it! He'll get over it.';
- Questioning and Probing—the intent is to gain additional information but which may turn into an interrogation such as 'Did she have a disturbed night? Did anything unusual happen this morning? Is everything alright at home?'; and
- Understanding or Reflecting—the listener's response focuses on the underlying feelings as well as the content and indicates her understanding of the message to the speaker in a short paraphrase such as 'You're concerned about Sam's adjustment to child-care' or 'You appear to be pretty pleased with how the program is developing!'.

Rogers argued that, of the five response types, the Understanding or Reflecting response was the most underdeveloped and underused with professionals frequently and indiscriminately utilising the remaining four. The other four response types, while appropriate at times, can have a detrimental effect upon communication if they are insensitively applied. They also contain inherent disadvantages as an initial response in a communication exchange because they do not acknowledge the speaker's feelings, allow for the possibility of clarification of meaning or communicate that the intended full meaning of the message has been understood. The Understanding or Reflecting response, in addition to overcoming these limitations, enables the speaker to explore the issue in greater depth and can be used to empower individuals to solve their own problems without having to rely on the expert professional. This is an important consideration for early childhood professionals whose role and responsibilities include supporting the personal development of parents and the professional development of staff.

Effective leaders in early childhood contexts will be aware of the advantages and limitations of the different response types and use their experience and expertise to determine which would be the most productive for meeting others' needs in the situation. The appropriateness of response type is the hallmark of a highly sophisticated and competent professional communicator.

Managing feelings

It has been suggested that 'people professions' are the most emotionally arousing and stress prone occupations in today's society (Bailey, 1986; Cherniss, 1995). Early childhood leaders spend their working day immersed in people, their expectations, needs, problems and demands and consequently are required to respond to and deal with situations which can elicit emotional reactions on their part. While it is important to recognise and articulate personal reactions and emotional responses to events in our professional lives, it is essential that these are managed in a professional manner which does not affect early childhood practitioners' ability to meet the needs of others and which does not diminish others' sense of self-esteem.

Early childhood services are dominated by women. Women in Western societies have tended to be socialised to take the role of placator in emotionally arousing situations. In general, they tend to have difficulty acknowledging the legitimacy of their emotions and expressing them in a constructive manner. The usual tendency is to deny and bury feelings until they build up to explosion point. There have been many anecdotal reports of early childhood staff avoiding issues by storming out, slamming doors, crying, name calling, blaming and absenting themselves from work until 'things calm down'. It seems that it is still more the exception than the rule that women in the early childhood field confront emotionally arousing incidents in an assertive manner. To add to this difficulty, early childhood leaders interact with a diverse group of people such as babies, toddlers and pre-schoolers, younger and older parents and staff as well as professionals from other organisations who are pursuing their own agendas, who differ in their ability to manage their own emotions and who are experiencing various levels of stress and vulnerability in their personal lives.

The effective leader in early childhood will be aware of the potential for emotional arousal in the interdependence of the group of children, parents and staff, and will understand the need to accept the emotional responses of other people. She will respond to these on a genuine and professional level and be

42

aware of her personal biases, resources and skills for managing her own feelings in the workplace. This is the point where the connection between meeting others' needs and meeting our own needs is made. In order to manage our own feelings in the professional situation, the early childhood practitioner must develop skills to meet her own needs.

Skills for meeting our own needs

The early childhood profession has its roots in the tradition of philanthropy where the pioneer women who became involved in shaping the lives of young children were interested in understanding child development and how to promote it in order to rescue children from moral, spiritual and economic slums (Finkelstein, 1988), that is, they were interested in meeting the needs of others. Their motivation to act as advocates for child rearing, mothers and motherhood also stemmed from their desire to enhance the development and quality of their own moral, spiritual and intellectual lives, in other words, to meet their own needs. It appears that, as the early childhood movement failed to achieve professional credibility in the community commensurate with its history and achievements, the present focus on nurturing, unselfishness and improving the quality of children's environments has been given undue prominence and used to absolve practitioners from their responsibility for meeting their own needs for economic and political improvement. In other words, early childhood practitioners have come to perceive themselves as powerless to meet their own professional needs. They have sublimated their own needs into an almost evangelical crusade to meet the needs of others, such as children, parents and staff. The dual goals held by the pioneer women should be restored for present early childhood practitioners so that they can have their own needs as professionals met as well as meet the needs of the consumers of their services.

Part of the ability to meet our own needs lies in the concept of self and self-esteem which have been discussed earlier in this chapter. Early childhood leaders need to be able to value their occupation and its contribution to society and have a realistic assessment of their own strengths and limitations in order to meet others' and their own needs. If an early childhood practitioner perceives herself or her job as inferior, inadequate or less worthy than other people or jobs, this will result in a loss of confidence about perceived and actual requirements which are necessary to fulfil professional roles and responsibilities.

The tendency of early childhood practitioners towards nurturing and meeting the needs of others has resulted in the phenomenon of burnout which initially was reported by Jorde-Boom (1982) and continues to be identified by members of the field. Burnout can result from meeting the needs of others at the expense of one's own needs. Burnout leads to reduced performance, staff absenteeism and staff turnover, all of which diminish the quality of early childhood services (Ryan, 1989). One way of avoiding this is to ensure that a balance is created between meeting the needs of others and meeting our own needs. Assertion is a skill which permits people to do this in a constructive way.

Appropriate self-assertion

The most important skill that early childhood leaders can develop both for themselves and for the consumers of their services is appropriate self-assertion. This skill is useful in situations such as setting limits with children, communicating a request to a parent, expressing an opinion to a staff member, setting parameters with a committee, meeting their own needs to express feelings appropriately, being honest in responses to other people and asking not to be interrupted. It is important for other people with whom leaders interact because it is a skill that enables effective communication in ways which preserve others' sense of self-esteem. Kotzman (1989) provides an informative and comprehensive overview of assertive behaviour.

What is assertion? Very simply, assertion is a matter-of-fact statement that conveys rights, opinions, beliefs, desires and positive or negative feelings in a way that does not impact on the self-esteem of the other person (Alberti & Emmons, 1970). It is a professional technique for communicating with other people because it is a direct and honest expression which conveys personal confidence and respect for self and others. Being assertive does not guarantee that individuals get what they want. What it does do is enhance the professional relationship by being emotionally honest, confronting issues and problems and respecting the fact that other people are responsible for managing their own feelings and responses.

Assertion (or using fair play) is the position of balance between two other familiar behaviours: non-assertion (avoiding conflict) and aggression (winning at all costs). These three communication styles can be seen as a continuum from the passive, indirect, self-denying non-assertive style to the confronting, inappropriately emotionally-honest and self-enhancing at others' expense, aggressive style. Both non-assertion and aggression can have negative and destructive effects upon further communication and ultimately in terms of future relationships, whereas assertion is considered to act as a facilitator to further communication and assists in building and maintaining relationships as well as personal confidence and self-esteem.

Most people have some difficulty in communicating assertively, either in certain situations or with certain people. Few people possess the level of self-confidence and skill necessary for consistent self-assertion. Inability to act assertively usually is related to lack of self-esteem where our own needs are undervalued in relation to others' needs and consequently denied. Or, on the other hand, our own needs are perceived as dominant and superior to those of others and self-righteously, aggressively pursued.

These differences explain why individuals can be seen to fluctuate between the three communication styles described above. For example, a person may be able to assert herself with young children when being interrupted by saying something like 'Excuse me, John, I'd like to finish talking to Susan'. The same person might have difficulty being assertive in a similar situation with John's mother and may respond non-assertively by permitting herself to be interrupted. It is likely that negative feelings of hurt, anxiety and guilt for not taking responsibility for one's own needs will be experienced later. Those individuals who persistently engage in non-assertive behaviour can build up levels of frustration which ultimately result in an aggressive outburst, that is, the mouse turns into a lion and intimidates a surprised recipient of the emotional eruption. On the other hand, the same person may only be able to confront an issue which is of concern to them by fuelling themselves first with anger. For example, the person may confront the issue of being interrupted by another staff member with an aggressive response such as, 'Well, that's just typical of you! You never let anyone finish what they are saying. I'm just not going to bother any more!'. The person on the receiving end of this outburst is likely to feel attacked, angry and vengeful, which will affect the relationship at a later time.

In a professional setting, early childhood practitioners need to analyse their own obstacles to appropriate self-assertion. Continued non-assertion and disregard for personal needs might be a symptom of poor self-concept and low self-esteem and will generally lead to anxiety and frustration. A tendency towards aggressive responses which infringe upon the rights of others also reflects problems with unrealistically inflated or poor self-concept and self-esteem and will lead to unmanageable relationships in the workplace. Individuals who are uncertain about their ability to be assertive in specific situations or with certain people usually do not believe that they are entitled to basic personal rights. In order to increase one's confidence in such situations, an examination of one's belief system in relation to personal rights is useful. All human beings have the right to make decisions about their body, property, and time and be treated with respect by others. In addition, we all have the right to express appropriately our own opinions, feelings and wishes.

Another obstacle to appropriate self-assertion is fear of the consequences of assertive behaviour. Non-assertive individuals usually believe that people will not like them or will reject them if they express their feelings. In fact, the opposite is true. People generally respond well to assertive individuals and feel irritated with, pity for and ultimately disgust for chronically non-assertive individuals. Aggressive individuals usually believe that the use of power achieves the goal in relationships. This may appear so in the short term where individuals may defer to the demands of the aggressive person. However, the long-term consequences of aggression are that the support, cooperation and goodwill of the recipients of aggressive displays are lost and a desire to take revenge, get even and retaliate can emerge. This negative reaction can escalate into situations where the aim is to sabotage.

Assertive responses are usually appropriate for situations which occur frequently and with people with whom one wishes to continue a positive relationship. Therefore, there are usually many opportunities to practise assertive responses and to learn from the results. Learning any new skill takes time and practice and learning to act assertively is no different. In order to be appropriately assertive in early childhood professional situations, the following steps can be followed:

1 Identify what you actually want to accomplish, that is, the goal of the assertive situation. For example, you may wish to have a particular parent pay his fees on time each week.
2 Clarify how being assertive will help you achieve this. In this

instance, being assertive will permit you to explain your needs in the situation, such as the budget requirements.

3 Analyse what you would usually do to avoid being assertive in this situation or with this person. In the past, you may have sent a note home with the child, left messages on the parent's answering machine or dropped subtle hints.

4 Clarify what the likely advantages of being assertive instead would be. The direct expression of your needs and wishes will minimise misinterpretation and misunderstanding of your requirements and maximise the probability of the parent responding to your request to pay the fees on time.

5 Identify what might be preventing you from being assertive here. Are you holding false notions about the consequences of being assertive? Could it be that your non-assertion is related to mistaken beliefs about the need for politeness in interactions about money? Do you fear an aggressive or tearful response from the parent?

6 Identify any other sources of anxiety and think of how you will cope with and reduce them. Are you anxious about what the parent might say about you to the staff or other parents? Think about and reaffirm your own rights in the situation.

7 Construct a model response that you would feel comfortable saying in the situation or to the person and practise it aloud several times. Refine the statement if necessary until you find one that feels genuine. You could say something like, 'I need to speak to you about the payment of fees. When the fees are not paid on time I become concerned that the centre will not have sufficient funds to meet its operational demands. I'd prefer it if you could let me know if your fees cannot be paid on time. That will give me time to assess my budget and give us an opportunity to negotiate some alternatives'.

8 When the situation arises, have the courage to put into practice your assertive response knowing that you will probably have another opportunity to try again.

9 Reflect upon the results of your assertive statement in terms of what you liked about what you did, the outcome and what you would change in the next opportunity to be assertive. You may have liked that you were direct, explained your needs and responsibilities, that you stayed calm and didn't attack the parent or that you opened up a chance for further discussion.

Using these steps will help achieve the goal of assertiveness and increase self-confidence in managing the communication exchange. The way in which the assertive statement is phrased is the next important skill in meeting your own needs.

'I' messages

The aim of communicating assertively is to express honestly and directly personal opinions, feelings and wishes. Unfortunately, particularly when emotions are aroused, personal opinions can be turned into statements of blame which are not conducive to productive relationships and can act as barriers to further communication. The use of 'you' to begin statements may arouse defensive tendencies and provoke a retaliatory attack. Consider the effects of these two statements on a staff member when you want to discuss the issue of punctual return from tea breaks. 'You're late back from tea again, Joan. You've got us all behind in the lunch routine! This better not happen again!' An alternative is: 'I'm concerned about the effect of our breaks on the lunchtime routines, Joan. I'd like to discuss the issue when you've got some time.'

The first statement puts the blame for the problem squarely on Joan in a fairly threatening way and does not lay any groundwork for problem solving. Joan is likely to react in a defensive manner, become angry at the attack and find reasons why the problem is nothing to do with her but with other issues about which the speaker is obviously ignorant. In the second statement, the speaker is able to employ a matter of fact tone of voice to define the issue at point of discussion and provide a non-threatening framework to explore with Joan what factors could be contributing to the issue. Joan is less likely to perceive herself as the focus of blame and attack and therefore more likely to discuss the issue openly and constructively.

In terms of owning personal statements, it is important to commence sentences and statements with the 'I' pronoun rather than generalised terms such as 'we', 'they' or 'some parents'. This subtle change in emphasis eliminates emotional overtones which can impede clear communication and reduces the likelihood of petty disputes about the source and intent of the message. The 'I' message allows the appropriate expression of feelings in a professional context such as, 'I was annoyed to find that the kitchen was not cleaned after the staff meeting last night. I'd prefer it if we could come up with a satisfactory arrangement for the next meeting'. Using this framework, the early childhood professional can address issues and express opinions in a constructive manner and provide a model for professional communication exchanges in the centre.

Conflict resolution

Conflict appears to be an inevitable part of living and working with other people and because the early childhood profession is essentially about working with people, the potential for conflict is high. The large number of requests from professionals in early childhood settings for assistance in dealing with and managing conflict indicates that this is an area of concern for their own personal 'survival' and job satisfaction. It is an area where early childhood professionals regard themselves as having little skill. Conflict management will be discussed in detail in Chapter 3.

Delegation

One of the biggest problems that early childhood professionals report is the amount and diversity of the work which is required in order to fulfil their roles and responsibilities. In terms of completing the workload, the effective leader will know when and how to delegate work to others so that the goals of the service are achieved.

Delegation is a skill. It is not simply asking or directing a staff member to complete a task. Delegation requires a match between the task to be undertaken and the skills, interests and characteristics of the staff member perceived as an appropriate delegatee. In order to delegate successfully, the early childhood professional has to be willing to relinquish some of the duties and responsibilities that have previously been associated with her role. It is important that the tasks considered appropriate to assign to other staff include some of the pleasant, rewarding jobs as well as some of the more mundane and unpleasant jobs. Delegation is not getting rid of all the tasks which are unpleasant, unpopular or boring.

Delegation involves having confidence in the staff and their ability to act as responsible professionals. Neugebauer (1983) provides a framework for assessing 'delegation phobia' and guidelines for effective delegation. The delegator needs a clear understanding of the relative importance of the various tasks which are considered suitable for delegation and be able to distinguish between key leadership functions which should always be retained by the leader (such as evaluation, policy development and reports for the committee of management) and other duties which could be undertaken by others (such as fee subsidies, petty cash and organising in-service programs).

There are two important issues in delegation: the selection of the appropriate person to delegate to and the way in which the nature of the task is communicated to them. When selecting the appropriate person to undertake a specific task, the early childhood leader needs know the potential of the staff by being familiar with their strengths, weaknesses, personal characteristics and learning styles and their work aspirations. Maslow's theory (1970) which proposed The Hierarchy of Needs (George & Cole, 1992) is useful to understand why individual staff members come to work, their predominant motivation and their potential to undertake special delegated tasks.

Maslow's (1970) framework for understanding people's motivation describes lower level needs which, if fulfilled, permit the individual to progress to higher order needs. At the lowest level are physiological needs, such as the need for food, water and sleep. The financial remuneration gained through employment enables these needs to be met and is a basic motivation for all workers regardless of how much they earn. When these physiological needs are met, the individual is able to pursue fulfillment at the next level of need, that is, safety needs. At this level, the worker is motivated by needs for security, stability, structure, law and order, protection and freedom from fear and anxiety. Casual employment status, such as casual relief work in early childhood settings, is unlikely to assist in meeting these needs. The employee will be interested in undertaking tasks that are perceived to contribute to her personal safety and security such as meeting minimum work expectations and competency, detailing rosters of who is responsible for what tasks and any other activities that ensure predictability in the work environment and the continuation of employment.

Maslow's third level is characterised by belonging and love needs, where individuals are motivated to work in order to be part of a group, to extend their social network and to meet needs for affectionate relationships with others. Such individuals will be interested in tasks that build and maintain relationships. These will be the people who will arrange the Christmas party, suggest staff dinners and organise the afternoon tea for staff farewells. Their need for harmonious relationships means that they may also take on the role of mediator when conflict between staff occurs or relationships are strained.

Maslow's fourth and fifth levels in the Hierarchy of Needs describe motivation typologies that are relevant to efficient delegation of important responsibilities. The need for esteem is the dominant motivator in relation to work at the fourth level. There appear to be two sub-levels of this need. Firstly, individuals are motivated by the need to demonstrate mastery, competence, autonomy and self-confidence and secondly, a need to feel appreciated and important and to gain a sense of respect from others emerges. Status, prestige and perhaps even fame become dominant motivators. Individuals who wish to demonstrate their competence and gain public recognition for a job well done will respond well to delegation particularly if the task is introduced with the phrase, 'I think you are the best person to undertake this important task'. However, if the task is perceived to be beyond the personal capability of the staff member and there is a chance of failure, it is unlikely that the individual will accept the delegation. Assurance from the leader about access to support and assistance if required may help convince a staff member to undertake the task.

The highest level of Maslow's Hierarchy of Needs is described as the need for self-actualisation. This is the level where the individual is motivated by the need for personal growth and development. Individuals at this level work because they want to develop their potential and become the best that they can be. This is the level where the greatest differences between individuals are evident. In terms of delegation, individuals at this level will be interested in challenging tasks which may demand the acquisition of new skills or knowledge. The individual at this level is truly a 'Learning Person', which has been referred to earlier in this chapter. The main difference between this level and the previous level is the role of demonstrated competence and public recognition versus personal standards of achievement, success and growth. A staff member's contribution is a result of intrinsic motivation rather than factors external to the self.

The effective early childhood leader will consider individual staff members' motivation in relation to their employment and match this with the kind and level of task deemed suitable for delegation. Having decided that a particular task is suitable for delegation and then selecting a potential delegatee on the basis of characteristics, skills, interests and motivation type, the leader needs to invite the staff member to undertake the task. It is important that the leader explain the nature of the task to be undertaken, the deadline by which the task must be completed, the level of authority and accountability that will be assigned to the person who undertakes the task, and finally the reasons why the staff member is considered to be the best person for the job. The leader should also ask for some input from the staff member concerning any aspect associated with the performance and completion of the task. In effective delegation, the leader needs to explicitly define her role as one of support and facilitation rather than one of supervision. A time line and procedures for reporting back should be decided upon as well as a means of evaluating the work.

In delegating tasks and duties to other staff members, it is important for the early childhood leader to keep in mind that other people are likely to approach and complete the job differently from the way that she would have. Therefore, reasonable expectations of others and the final outcome are essential if staff are to perceive delegation as a means of staff development and a pathway to job satisfaction. Inappropriate delegation can lead staff to feel exploited, misunderstood and frustrated in their work. It can also result in the early childhood leader losing confidence in the staff and herself and retreating to the unproductive position of, 'If you want a job done well, then you have to do it yourself'. Delegation should result in an improvement of the morale and performance of the entire staff as well as ensuring that there is sufficient time for the early childhood leader to devote to her own work. If time is still a problem, then time management strategies need to be investigated.

Time management

One of the most pressing problems facing early childhood professionals today is insufficient time to complete the range of responsibilities which are associated with delivering services for young children and their families. Yet, when the topic of time management is mentioned to early childhood practitioners, the response is usually one of scepticism. It is evident that the demands of the jobs of coordinators and directors of early childhood centres have increased dramatically over the past decade and, with the ongoing changes in the early childhood field, this trend seems likely to continue. Although many of the paperwork tasks can be taken home and completed outside work time, the impact of such a practice conducted on a regular basis is likely to be destructive in terms of increased personal stress levels and less time for family life. While the work may get done, it is often at a personal cost to the leader. The effects of poor time management will be taken up in the next section on stress management.

Time management is simply a strategy which can be used to assist early childhood practitioners meet all the demands that are placed upon them during a typical day. It must be remembered that there are also many activities which take place during the evening and on weekends, such as evening staff meetings, week-end workshops and conferences, fund-raising functions and centre maintenance work parties. A forty hour working week is not the norm for those who work in early childhood services. In addition, because early childhood staff are 'public figures' in that their performance is observable by the consumers of their service, it is essential that they be seen to handle the variety of demands on their time and also do this in a manner which presents an image of competence and efficiency. At this point, a distinction needs to be made between 'being busy' and 'being efficient'. A 'busy' leader might well analyse her willingness to delegate some of her duties and responsibilities to other appropriate staff. It may well be that the leader's delegation phobia (Neugebauer, 1983) is interfering with efficient task accomplishment and leadership.

Time management is merely a means of getting things done as quickly as possible and with as little stress as possible. It essentially involves setting goals in one's personal and professional life and establishing priorities for the tasks which are to be undertaken in order to achieve these goals. The major obstacle to time management in early childhood services is interruption. Therefore, skill in dealing with this problem must be developed. Appropriate self-assertion which has been discussed earlier in this chapter is useful here. If an early childhood leader manages her time efficiently, the result should be more time available to work towards achieving set goals without feelings of stress or pressure.

Time management involves four major steps according to Schiller and Dyke (1990):

1 Set your goals (in work, professional development, personal growth, and material areas). It is useful to break these up into long and short-term goals.
2 Analyse which task or project will help you reach the particular goal.

3   Break the task or project down into small, achievable steps.
    Evidence of progress towards the goal is a good motivator!
4   Establish a priority rating. Which task needs to be completed
    first to move towards the goal?

There are some helpful tips in time management and general
organisational efficiency. Although this seems an obvious strategy,
it is important to remember that lists are useful to help you plan
each day, week or month. General headings, such as Things To
Do, People To See, Phone Calls To Make, Meetings To Attend,
Deadlines To Make, can focus your attention on the demands on
your time and can assist with establishing priorities for tasks. As
you complete each task, cross it off the list. If a task remains
unfinished, analyse why it has not been completed. Did you have
enough time, were there too many interruptions, weren't you
interested in it, was it too difficult, did you have all the information
necessary, is the morning better than the afternoon for complex
report writing, was this a task which could have been delegated?

Effective organisation of office space tends to be associated
with efficient use of time. The early childhood coordinator's or
director's office space is a multi-purpose space often doubling as
a store room, staff room, resource library, parent room, interview
room and time-out room. It may not be easy to keep it in perfect
order. However, the more chaos and clutter in the office, the less
accessible it is for efficient use of time. The creation of a workable
filing system is essential to handle the amount of information that
comes through to leaders of early childhood services. A computer
is an essential item of equipment which can ease the administrative
load. The time initially spent learning to use the computer will
produce considerable savings later, particularly when compared
with manual handling of paperwork.

Telephone calls are reported to be a major source of stress in
the lives of early childhood practitioners. The telephone is an
important link between the centre and the outside world especially
in the present security conscious environment. Parents also have
the right to contact staff about their child at any time. It is not
the telephone itself that is the problem. It is people's poor
telephone skills that give rise to problems. The most important
strategies are to keep incoming and outgoing telephone calls short,
to ensure that you have communicated accurately the purpose of
your call, to make all necessary calls in one session and to
consider whether some calls can be handled by other staff. Finding
a way of freeing yourself from answering the telephone and

creating an uninterrupted period of time to complete an important task is essential.

Meetings can be another source of inefficient usage of time. Meetings seem to abound in the early childhood field and, because early childhood centres tend to be physically remote from the administrative offices in which meetings are conducted, the time needed to attend a one hour meeting can easily amount to two hours with associated travelling time. The early childhood leader who uses time efficiently will assess the need to hold or attend a meeting in terms of the goals of the centre. Only those people who are relevant to the purpose of the meeting should be invited and the person who chairs the meeting should ensure that the discussion focuses on the topic. Learning some techniques for chairing group meetings can be valuable if meetings make up a substantial part of your duties and can assist with the effective management of time.

It is evident that, with the increasing roles and responsibilities that early childhood practitioners are required to undertake, a change of mind set is necessary. Early childhood practitioners need to learn ways of working smarter not harder.

Stress management

The pressure of time is only one of a number of stressful factors that are associated with working in the early childhood field. Working with young children is physically, emotionally and intellectually demanding. Families appear to face considerable pressures associated with the demands of contemporary living. The scope of the early childhood practitioner's job has broadened to include a wide range of responsibilities. Among these are working with young children, supporting parents in their parenting role, training centre staff, working with other professionals in relation to children's needs, and acting as advocates for children, families and the profession. Many of the recent changes in the roles and responsibilities of early childhood practitioners have not been supported by access to relevant training with numerous early childhood staff having to 'learn on the job'. Given the staff:child ratio which is required for early childhood services by government regulations, it can be difficult for staff to gain time off or be relieved from duty in order to attend training courses, many of which are offered during the hours that early childhood centres are open. It is therefore common for early childhood professionals who do engage in further study and training, to have to undertake pre-service, in-service and post-initial training in their own time. This demand can affect the quality of their personal lives and result in increased stress levels.

Stress is part of modern life and work and, as such, it is unrealistic to expect that stress can be eliminated totally. However, stress can be managed by either changing the situation or changing ourselves. Stress is somewhat self-induced in that it is a product of the balance between the number of demands in our lives and our individual perceptions regarding our capacity or resources to meet these demands (Bailey, 1986). In the case of many early childhood professionals, the demands often outweigh personal resources with stress being the result of this imbalance. While time management and delegation can assist with the reduction of stress levels in the professional arena, a broader strategy for approaching stress in all aspects of our lives is more useful.

Stress levels determine our effectiveness in both our personal and professional lives. Too much stress or overstimulation tends to produce irrational problem solving, low self-esteem, physical exhaustion and illness, all of which result in low quality performance in the workplace. Lack of stress or understimulation can have an equally negative impact on coping strategies with boredom, fatigue, frustration and dissatisfaction reducing professional effectiveness. Neither of these extremes meets the needs of others or our own needs. With an optimum level of stimulation or challenge, early childhood professionals can demonstrate their capacity for rational problem solving and creativity which produces a positive attitude to progress and change and enhances self-esteem and job satisfaction. With such a balance, it is possible to meet our own needs as well as be responsive to the needs of others. However, achieving this balance requires self-understanding, an understanding of work demands and continued effort to keep both of these in perspective.

The first step in managing stress in personal and professional arenas is to determine who and what is causing the stress. In other words, a stress inventory which lists all the people and situations that are associated with feeling stressed needs to be compiled. A stress inventory also permits reflection upon typical coping strategies and an evaluation of their effectiveness.

The following steps are helpful in analysing the main causes of stress:

1 Briefly describe the stressful situation. For example, a confer-

ence with a parent concerning their child's unacceptable behaviour.

2   Identify who is involved in the situation.

3   Establish how frequently this situation occurs. Conferences with parents occur frequently, on a weekly basis with some parents.

4   Determine the degree of control you have over the situation and/or people involved. In such a case, you consider that you have some ability to influence parents' attitudes and behaviour.

5   Identify typical ways of responding to or dealing with the situation. When you encounter stressful situations, you tend to ignore them, hope the problem will resolve itself without your intervention or avoid direct confrontation by dropping hints around the parents.

6   Evaluate how effective these strategies are for accomplishing your work and maintaining positive relationships. In your past experience, you have found such non-assertive strategies to be ineffective but you are too anxious to try anything new.

7   Brainstorm possible alternative ways of dealing with the situation in a more constructive manner for your own needs. Assertiveness training to help you express your needs and practice in mutual problem solving could be beneficial.

In meeting our need for a relatively stress free working environment, there are two important aspects to consider: how frequently the situation occurs and the degree of control over the situation. If a situation occurs frequently, it would seem that current coping strategies are not effective and require reviewing. Where situations cannot be changed because of the lack of personal control, exploring strategies for changing personal perceptions and thinking can be more productive than trying to change the situation. In the above example, rather than thinking that your ability to deal with parent conferences is hopeless, try changing your thinking to, 'I don't like parent conferences but I can cope with them. I can learn skills to help me feel more confident.'

Stress management strategies focus on either changing the situation or changing yourself. Most people are reluctant to engage in personal change if another option is available. Therefore, strategies for changing the situation will be discussed first.

In the early childhood profession, stress at work can be reduced by analysing and making minor or more substantial changes to the job. If stress is related to the demands of the job, then the workload needs to be reorganised. Some helpful techniques are:

- Reduce the workload. Delegate appropriate tasks to others. Other staff will benefit from and may even appreciate the opportunity to learn new skills. This provides another advantage in that additional backup is available if the leader is unable to be at work for any reason.
- Establish priorities for the demands placed upon you. Learn to be assertive, deal with only essential demands and avoid becoming involved in tasks which are peripheral to your role.
- Use and improve time management techniques to ensure that you use time as efficiently as possible.
- Assume control. There are always options in any situation. Avoiding situations will not resolve any difficulties but can exacerbate them. Make choices and decisions rather than being at the mercy of events.
- Finish any unfinished tasks before starting new ones. The sense of completion can quickly neutralise anxiety about the amount of work that has to be done.
- If possible, minimise change and keep to a routine. Stress is usually associated with the uncertainty of change. If stress is a result of chronic change, such as has been occurring in the early childhood field in recent years, routine, predictability and stability can build up self-esteem and nurture feelings of security.
- Seek and establish a support group. Avoid withdrawing from and possibly alienating colleagues, peers and friends. Stress is a common experience for early childhood professionals who therefore can empathise with each other when they feel overwhelmed by the demands and changes in the profession.

When early childhood professionals have little personal control over a stressful situation and cannot change the situation to ameliorate stress levels, it is possible to manage stress by changing the way the situation is perceived or viewed. The following personal stress antidotes may be helpful in changing the way we think about stressful situations:

- Change the perception held about stress in general. Rather than seeing stressful situations as things to be avoided in life, view these situations as challenges and opportunities for growth and personal development. Accept that it is not the situation but how the situation is perceived which produces stress.

- Change your thinking to less catastrophic, less extreme, less polarised, less stressed and therefore more positive and rational thinking. Use self talk to define situations. Self talk is simply an ability to listen to the internal messages we give ourselves about any particular event. Instead of thinking or saying 'Isn't this dreadful! I just can't stand any more!', try thinking something like 'Well, I don't like this very much but I can deal with it! I could . . .' In this way, the tendency to irrational, over-emotional thinking is limited without denying the basic emotional response. An opportunity to perceive the situation more realistically and to adopt a rational, problem-solving approach is provided.

- Learn to tolerate uncertainty in life. Not everything can be controlled, directed, planned or predicted. Learn to 'go with the flow' sometimes, particularly when you don't have the power to control events. Worrying will not improve or change the situation but will only increase your sense of uncertainty and your stress level.

- Don't dwell on past mistakes or in the past. Focus on how you can change the future because only the future can be changed.

- Learn to anticipate change. Working in a 'people profession' means that constant change is inevitable but there are usually numerous signs to alert you to the need for change or an imminent change. A perceptive professional will be attuned to signs of pending change, will plan for change and will facilitate the implementation of change in order to minimise stress in those affected by the change. Skills for managing change will be discussed in Chapter 6.

- Develop the skills necessary to perform your job efficiently. Attend in-service courses and upgrade your qualifications to ensure that you possess the current technical expertise demanded in the profession.

- Improve the communication skills which are related to stress management, in particular, assertion and conflict resolution skills. Express your feelings appropriately and deal with incidents as they occur.

In addition to the techniques described above, there are two basic strategies for stress management in personal and professional life. The first one relates to personal health and the second relates to relaxation. Because stress has an underlying physiological component, one's susceptibility to stress can be reduced by ensuring that good health is maintained. Any professional who wishes to function effectively needs to have a balanced diet, avoid or minimise the use of drugs (including caffeine, nicotine and alcohol), take regular exercise and have adequate sleep. This is especially important in professions which require physical, emotional and intellectual stamina such as the early childhood profession. Learning to relax and developing recreational interests are also means of ensuring psychological health and stamina.

In summary, an effective early childhood professional has a balanced personal and professional life which enables her to meet others' needs while ensuring that her needs are also met. This balance is a result of effective communication skills, the ability to delegate and to respond to conflict constructively as well as the capacity to manage time and personal stress effectively.

3

Conflict resolution

Conflict appears to be a phenomenon which characterises the psychological climate of early childhood services given the frequency and intensity of disagreements, arguments, quarrels and disputes which are reported by coordinators and directors of centres. What this conflict signifies is the breakdown of communication and interpersonal relationships in the group. Where a workplace depends on social interaction, conflict is inevitable. This is a serious problem for early childhood services because the basis of service provision is social interaction and harmonious relationships. In any service where group relationships are related to the achievement of goals or where the relationships need to be maintained in order to provide a service, skills for the management and resolution of conflict are essential. Early childhood professionals need to learn to approach conflict in a positive manner and deal with it in ways that strengthen group relationships.

Quality care and early education depend on the ability of the staff to work productively together towards achieving the centre's goals. The leader of the group needs to develop skills to assist the staff in confronting the problems which are likely to arise as staff work towards their goals. Anecdotal evidence from leaders of early childhood services indicates that some staff prefer to fight and compete rather than cooperate to achieve their goals. Unfortunately, many early childhood practitioners still regard conflict as an abnormal occurrence that is not supposed to happen if people get on reasonably well with one another. 'Why are we having all of these problems? What is wrong with our centre? Why can't we stop fighting and get on with the job?' are questions typically asked by early childhood staff who also tend to believe that their centre is the only one having problems. What is not understood is that these sorts of questions are inappropriate for the work situation and illustrate that conflict is a misunderstood phenomenon. Rather, conflict needs to be considered as a natural part of work and life. The situation would be more of concern if conflict were not occurring. The real issue is not that conflict exists but how it is approached and managed. The type of question that needs to be asked by early childhood professionals is 'Given that conflict is a normal part of the work experience, how are we going to handle it?'.

Conflict in early childhood settings is a form of interpersonal interaction in which two or more people struggle or compete over claims to beliefs, values, preferences, resources, power, status or any other desire. It is evident that the early childhood context provides a ripe arena for conflicts to emerge given that individual philosophies about caring for and educating young children are derived from subjective beliefs, values and preferences supported by personal experience. In fact, many early childhood staff have reported that dealing with conflict over ethical dilemmas is a major source of tension in the work place (Clyde & Rodd, 1989). All staff and parents will have their unique perspective on what is the best and therefore the only way to care for and educate young children, that is, their way. The right to relate to children on the basis of one's subjective philosophy regardless of the extent to which it is consistent with centre philosophy is often defended by parents and staff with emotional, irrational and inconsistent arguments.

It is obvious that uncontrolled or chronic conflict within work groups is harmful to both the quality of work and productivity as well as the quality of life and relationships. People spend their energy in dysfunctional ways, such as fighting, arguing, ridiculing each other, competing and using resources inappropriately when they need to be collaborating to provide a quality service for children and parents and a pleasant working environment for themselves. However, it must be remembered that it is not conflict itself which is the problem. Conflict only becomes unhealthy and unproductive when it is not dealt with effectively. In addition, conflicts which are not managed effectively may appear to be resolved but can re-emerge at the next point of tension in the group or in other forms. The fact that many early childhood leaders report continuous bickering, quarrels, minor conflicts and ongoing tension suggests that their attempts to deal with the problems are not getting to the source of the issue but are dealing with symptoms of other underlying, unrecognised problems.

Until recently, conflict in the workplace was regarded by workers and theorists alike to be negative, counterproductive and to be avoided if possible. Only negative outcomes were associated with conflict. It was considered to be a setback to the group, with statements such as 'It will take some time for us to get back on our feet!' signifying the negative outcome on work performance and 'Give her some time. She'll get over it!' illustrating the perceived negative impact on group relationships. Disharmony engendered by feelings of anger and competition was considered to stunt personal and professional development, weaken relationships, decrease flexibility and result in lowered performance and consequently was regarded as unhealthy. However, disharmony if handled sensitively and creatively does not always have a negative outcome for work groups. It gives rise to a theoretical reconsideration and reconceptualisation of the role and function of conflict in the workplace.

Fortunately, organisational and human relations theorists now have a better understanding of the role of conflict and argue that, given the right situation and timing, conflict has functional aspects. Conflict now is considered to have positive functions for work groups and is seen as an inevitable and necessary part of group process because it provides an impetus for learning, growth, development and change. Conflict signifies that there is life and activity in the group and offers an opportunity for healthy learning. It can stimulate increased interest and curiosity, expose underlying tensions and unsatisfied needs, create new channels of communication and, if managed appropriately, result in the resolution of issues, increased flexibility in performance and strengthened relationships within the group. The way in which conflict is managed can turn it from a perceived setback into a positive learning experience for the group.

Sources of conflict within early childhood settings

In order to approach conflict positively and manage it effectively in the workplace, the early childhood professional needs an understanding of the origin of the conflict—where and how it arose. The source of the conflict can provide guidelines for dealing appropriately with the conflict. Communication skills usually form the basis of conflict management but it is important to recognise that some conflicts in early childhood settings are a result of structural elements and therefore will be difficult to resolve.

Group structure

The physical environment of many early childhood settings contains certain structural constraints which can increase the likelihood of conflict occurring in comparison with other work settings. Firstly, the staff are usually allocated to work in smaller groupings in separate rooms which affects the ease of communication. The centre's team spirit can be decreased by staff forming allegiances to their sub-groupings, for example, the babies' room, the toddlers' room or the pre-schoolers' room. The fact that two or three staff members can be required to work closely together in relative isolation from other staff can lead to misperceptions of favouritism by the team leader, resentment about imagined benefits or privileges that staff in other rooms might receive and rumours about the team leader's attitude to performance in the various room teams.

Given that many early childhood centres operate for almost twelve hours every day and that consumer demand will require even more flexible hours of operation, early childhood staff are required to undertake shift work. This also affects the ease of communication between staff because there will be very few times when all staff are together (and free of responsibility) to discuss issues. Where information is passed on second-hand, there is a possibility of communication breakdown and misunderstanding which can lead to conflict. Staff breaks also need to be rostered to meet the minimum supervisory requirements for young children. Consequently, there is not even a common lunchtime in which to communicate as a group. Add to these constraints rostered days off and holidays and it becomes obvious that many factors exist which mitigate effective communication within the staff group and increase the likelihood of communication breakdown and conflict.

Time is an important issue in all early childhood services and there is usually insufficient funding to employ relievers to free individual staff members to attend meetings or to work in their small teams outside their allocated planning time. This means that anything extra such as staff meetings, in-service training or special curriculum planning meetings must be held in the evenings or during the weekend, that is, in the staff members' own time. Not all staff have developed a concept of professionalism where it is an accepted expectation that some of your own time will need to be devoted to work. Also, many staff have other responsibilities, such as their own family commitments. Consequently, not all staff are able to meet outside the opening hours of the centre in order to share information. Those that can are usually on a tight time schedule and want meetings to be held in as short a time as possible, which influences the depth of information sharing and discussion that can be achieved.

Even within normal working hours the potential for conflict due to communication breakdown is high. Staff have a responsibility for the safety and welfare of young children which entails constant and alert supervision. The staff members' attention needs to be focused on the children at all times. Therefore, it is difficult to discuss an issue which arises during the day between two or three members of staff because they are not able to give it their full attention. Lack of attention to a staff member's comment may be interpreted as lack of interest, selfishness or some other negative explanation about why the comment was not taken up and acted upon. The need to focus attention on the children means that sometimes adult staff members will not have their own needs met and, instead of being appropriately assertive, staff members may become angry and initiate disharmony in the group.

The contact between parents and staff in the dropping off and picking up routines can also be conducive to conflict where neither parent nor staff stop to consider the needs of the other adult in the situation. Usually dropping off and picking up is a hurried process because the parent and staff have other responsibilities to meet. Staff may feel disregarded, unappreciated and exploited by parents who do not respond to their request to discuss a particular aspect of the child's progress and later respond to the parent in an off-hand or deprecatory manner. Staff may evaluate and label the parent in stereotyped terms and in future relate to the parent in terms of this stereotype. It may only take a few such experiences before a staff member may generalise this prejudice to all parents which will result in very unsatisfactory relationships with parents who use the centre. Similarly, if a staff member does not immediately respond to a parent's request for attention, the parent may evaluate the staff member as insensitive, uncaring and unprofessional. These concerns may be discussed with other parents or the centre's leader which is likely to leave the staff member feeling vulnerable, exposed and angry with the parent's reaction. The fact that neither parents nor staff have appropriate time or physical surroundings to discuss concerns at dropping off and picking up times can lead to misunderstanding and conflict. The problem with finding alternative times outside normal centre hours has already been highlighted.

Early childhood professionals need to be aware that the way in which early childhood centres are set up can provide communication difficulties which can very easily flare into situations of conflict if they are not dealt with immediately and effectively. There may be very little that can be done about the group structure and the physical setting but staff and parents can be alerted to the potential difficulties that these factors can foster.

Goals and policies of the early childhood centre

Successful teams are characterised by a set of achievable goals which are understood and accepted by all. The same can be said of roles and responsibilities which need to be undertaken within a centre for its successful operation. Unfortunately, many early childhood staff teams have not had the opportunity to be involved in the development of goals, policies and job descriptions. Due to the uneven emergence of notions of professionalism, some early childhood teams do not consider this area to be part of their responsibility. However, all centres have some form of centre philosophy, statement of mission, aims and objectives and policies which determine the operation of the centre. Given that these may have been imposed by the leader or a committee of management, not all staff will agree with and accept such goals and policies.

Conflict regarding goals and policies can be overt (where a staff member or parent openly disputes the validity of a certain policy) or covert (where the policy is superficially or tacitly accepted but is not supported or complied with in terms of action). Overt verbal or behavioural disagreement with goals or policies is easier to deal with because the conflict is obvious and there is a possibility for problem solving. Covert disagreement can sabotage the implementation of goals and policies because people may verbally deny that there is a conflict and refuse to engage in discussion. The leader needs to be assertive about her concerns regarding the issue and encourage open problem solving to help resolve the issue.

Unwritten laws that develop as part of the history of certain early childhood centres can also provide the grounds for conflict. Given the high turnover of staff in early childhood centres, it is likely that some of the staff will have had experience with different ways of dealing with issues and of meeting staff needs. Confusion about the acceptability of certain practices, such as 'mental health' days can lead to tension and conflict. The potential for conflict arising out of such misunderstandings can be minimised if as many aspects of policy as possible are accessible to public scrutiny. Unwritten laws which are so-called 'common knowledge' can provide a rich source of inequality, discrimination and conflict between leaders, staff and parents.

The reason that conflict can spring from goals and policies is that they have a value basis. Part of the ethics of leadership which are discussed in Chapter 9 requires that, in relation to conflict, the leader makes decisions about and acts on the basis of a clear personal and professional value system. The early childhood profession is dominated by individual beliefs, values and perspectives which can have a strong emotional component. Understanding that not all people are likely to accept or agree with the goals and policies of the centre is important. Providing opportunities for discussion, the sharing of perspectives and regular review is also necessary to minimise conflict in this area.

Values

Many of the goals, policies and practice in the early childhood field are based on values. Value systems are individual and although certain values may be held in common with other people, each of us develops a unique set of values which are used as guidelines or standards for decision making and behaviour. Particularly when it comes to young children and families, each of us holds strong, personal, emotionally laden values which are used to make decisions about what we believe to be in the best interest of children.

The personal ideas, values and beliefs of early childhood professionals can be as influential on practice as professional value systems (Yonemura, 1986) particularly in the early stages of professional development (Vander Ven, 1988). It is not uncommon to find conflict between early childhood staff which is based on differing values systems and their relationship to practice in areas such as goals for children's behaviour, children's needs, group management, planning and organisation, materials, learning and development, children's characteristics, educational processes, educational play, evaluation and assessment and home and parents (Spodek, 1987). The leader in the early childhood setting will facilitate the clarification of value beliefs on practice and articulate the relevance of professional values while acknowledging the role of personal values in making decisions about children and families.

Australia, like many countries in the world, is a multicultural pluralist society in which specific cultural values demand as much respect as more generally held community values. The early childhood profession recognises children's rights to have their culture and its value system affirmed in care and educational contexts, and acknowledges parents' desires to have their children exposed to adults from their own culture while attending early childhood programs. However, this is another area where the potential for conflict is high. The values of specific cultures sometimes are quite different from those of the general Australian community and of the early childhood profession, for example, the status and privileges which are given to young male children compared with young female children in some cultures and the lack of respect accorded to female staff by fathers from particular societies. These legitimate cultural differences can lead to conflict between staff from various cultural groups and to conflict between staff and parents. Appreciation of the ethics of leadership discussed in Chapter 9 is important in guiding responses to conflicts which arise from different value systems.

Leadership style

The general characteristics pertaining to leadership styles have been described in detail in Chapter 1. However, it is important to understand that the general style of leadership employed by the early childhood centre's coordinator or director may influence the level of conflict experienced in a centre. The type of leadership style is sometimes related to the level of maturity and experience of the staff where, for example, young and less experienced staff may be responsive to a more directive style which, if used with mature and experienced staff, could produce antagonism and conflict.

Leaders who have a tendency to be authoritarian when making decisions and dealing with staff (such as Neugebauer's Task Master described in Chapter 1) may find that the level of conflict is higher in their centres than leaders who are more democratic and include staff participation in making decisions about matters which affect the operation of the centre. This appears to be due to the fact that most adults, particularly mature and experienced adults, resent being told what to do and think by someone else who does not recognise their expertise. Authoritarian leadership is likely to be most accepted by immature and inexperienced staff who are looking for direction and guidance in the workplace. However, as these people develop in confidence, they usually want to be more involved in matters that affect their work. A leader who does not change her style to match staff needs for involvement may inadvertently stimulate resentment and rebellion on the part of staff.

Authoritarian leaders can tend to take on the responsibility of acting as mediators in conflicts between various staff, and staff and parents, rather than facilitating the management of the conflict between the relevant parties. When the power hierarchy is invoked by either staff or parents to resolve disputes, one or both parties may be left feeling dissatisfied that their claims to justice were not given appropriate consideration and that resolution was imposed from outside. While the immediate issue may appear to be resolved, it is likely that any remaining underlying tension will re-emerge in another form or at another time. Early childhood professionals need to understand that conflict has to be worked through by those parties immediately affected with the leader demonstrating confidence that the parties themselves can reach a mutually acceptable solution. Support can be offered by modelling appropriate communication skills and discussion of alternatives in problem-solving sessions.

Permissive, 'anything goes' leadership (such as Neugebauer's Unleader outlined in Chapter 1) does not avoid the problem of conflict in early childhood centres. Leaders who do not provide direction and guidance, who accept poor quality performance from staff, who not not provide constructive feedback and who do not communicate high expectations of staff and parents will also find tension, resentment and disagreement among staff and parents. This type of leadership communicates a lack of respect and regard for children, parents, staff and the early childhood profession. Typically, lack of concern for the rights and needs of individuals, lack of tolerance and subjective prejudices will cause conflicts where there are few standards to act as guidelines for staff and parents.

A democratic leader (which is similar to Neugebauer's Motivator outlined in Chapter 1) will understand that conflict in the early childhood centre is a symptom of a breakdown in communication and interpersonal relationships and will involve relevant staff in an egalitarian process of problem solving. This collaborative style of leadership is likely to result in issues being addressed by the relevant people before they develop into larger problems. In this way, fewer problems are likely to develop into full-blown conflicts because they are dealt with as they arise. It is not the case that centres who have leaders with democratic or collaborative styles of leadership are less conflict prone, rather that the conflicts are approached and managed differently. The techniques for effective management of conflict will be discussed later in this chapter.

Job expectations and demands

One important aspect of leadership style is the degree of definition provided by leaders concerning job expectations and demands. Over-definition and leader-domination of job expectations and demands can diminish staff motivation and initiative. On the other hand, where roles and responsibilities have not been clearly defined and accepted as part of the team-building process, staff uncertainty and ambiguity about where responsibility lies can lead to disputes. Job expectations can be formed on the basis of previous experience or be derived from personal preference and presumption. Expectations derived from such sources may not be appropriate or relevant for the current situation. Therefore, it is essential that the leader provide opportunities for staff to clarify and negotiate who is responsible for what task or job.

Failure to articulate performance expectations for staff can also lead to tension and eventually conflict where staff can argue that 'I didn't know that you wanted it done that way!' or 'We didn't have to do it at the other centre! The coordinator always did it herself!'. People can experience stress in situations where expectations and demands are not clear. Stress may be dealt with by staff becoming defensive and blaming the leader for not adequately informing them of what was required. Therefore, in order to avoid this source of conflict, the perceptive leader will ensure that all staff members (and parents if necessary) clearly understand what is expected from them in the early childhood centre.

Employee distrust of authority

The leadership styles of some early childhood coordinators or directors can suggest to employees that the leader does not have the best interest or the welfare of the group at heart. The autocratic or Task Master style of leadership which is examined in Chapter 1 can produce such suspicions in staff members. Uncertainty regarding the motivation of the leader for certain actions can arouse negative attitudes towards the leader and result in lack of cooperation by staff members. For example, the introduction of staff appraisal by a leader who is not trusted by the staff is unlikely to be met with a positive response. Staff may perceive staff appraisal in negative terms, such as the leader wanting to terminate the employment of one or more staff members, whereas the leader actually may want to introduce a program of staff development based upon mutually agreed goals.

Where staff members distrust the leader and her motivation in the administration of the centre, staff are unlikely to support and participate in initiatives suggested by the leader. If the source of conflict appears to stem from this source, the leader needs to work on developing basic trust between herself and the staff members, ensuring that staff members have access to as much information as possible where policy and practical decision making are involved. In addition, staff participation in decision making and problem solving can help overcome employee distrust of the leader.

Inability to accept feedback or criticism on performance

One of the characteristics of effective communicators, and therefore of effective leaders, is their skill in delivering constructive feedback on staff performance. While many people understand feedback in terms of the negative aspect of criticism, the term 'feedback' also encompasses the positive aspect, that is, compliments and encouraging statements. The mistake many leaders make is to focus on the critical aspect and communicate personal blame to the individual staff member for not accomplishing a desired or expected outcome.

Probably due to the demands on their time and attention, few leaders consistently encourage staff by commenting on the aspects of the day which have gone well, their strengths and assets, their contribution to the centre or the areas in which they have improved. For example, instead of saying 'You haven't included adequate information in your outdoor plans' the leader could say 'I can see that you've put a lot of effort into your planning this week. I'm a little concerned about the lack of detail for the outdoor experiences. Could we find a time to discuss the outdoor aspect?' Alternatively, the leader might make encouraging comments such as 'I notice that you've improved considerably in writing objectives for individual children', 'I really appreciated your contribution to the discussion on next week's plans at the staff meeting this morning' or 'Since you've been writing fuller plans, I've noticed that the program seems to be running more smoothly in your room'.

If leaders focus on the critical rather than the encouraging aspect of feedback, staff can learn only to expect a negative appraisal by leaders when the word 'feedback' is mentioned. Consequently, staff will take a defensive attitude to any feedback from the leader. They may think that they need to defend themselves from the leader's supposed attack on their competence with a justification about why they did what they did. In some ways, staff inability to receive feedback is a function of their previous negative experience with feedback and criticism from leaders.

However, if a leader can phrase feedback in a way that does not arouse staff defensiveness and opens channels for further communication, feedback can become a means of facilitating staff development rather than a point of contention between the staff member and leader. Comments such as 'I noticed that you had set up a music experience which the children appeared to find very enjoyable. Can we get together to explore ways that you might extend Simon's participation? He seemed to be only peripherally involved'. Assisting staff to become familiar with constructive feedback which is phrased in an understanding and supportive style can avoid arguments in this area where staff believe that the leader has little understanding of and empathy for their position.

The introduction of regular staff appraisals for both leader and staff members in early childhood centres where aspects of professional growth and development are acknowledged, as well as setting goals for future improvement is one way of assisting staff to learn the role of feedback and how to accept and use it constructively.

Information and misinformation

In terms of the effective running of an early childhood centre, the importance of accurate and unambiguous communication and the potential for communication breakdown have been highlighted. Another issue in the area of communication is the basis upon which information is shared, that is, 'who has access to what information'. Early childhood professionals need to be aware that information is power. Those who possess information relevant to a particular situation are in a better position to protect and provide for themselves, to make better decisions and to demonstrate competent performance. In other words, information empowers people. Lack of information has the opposite effect.

Ethical considerations also affect what information is shared with whom. The early childhood professional will come across many situations where ethical dilemmas arise in terms of whether information is made available or withheld, for example, requests for information from social workers or the Family Court counsellors, requests for information from access parents, requests for information from other parents about children who bite or hit and the issue of reporting suspected child abuse. The early childhood professional is required to bring sensitivity, discretion and professional expertise and ethics to her decisions. In human relationships, very few decisions are clear-cut and can result in conflict if they have not been fully thought out. The use of a code of ethics for guiding teachers in ambiguous situations is discussed in Chapter 9.

Effective and respected leaders collaborate with others. They are willing to share information openly and do not use the sharing and withholding of information as means of wielding power in the centre. This is an important issue because much information comes directly to the coordinator or director of a centre who then has sole responsibility to make decisions about to whom and how that information will be disseminated. Staff who believe that they are being kept uninformed or denied access to information essential for them to perform their roles and responsibilities will be likely to lose confidence in the leader and perhaps ascribe negative motivation to such action.

Parents believe that they have the right to information available concerning their child and will quickly lose trust in an early childhood professional who does not provide them with what they regard as important information. The effective early childhood leader will need to use discretion about the information which is provided to parents simply because the majority of parents are not trained to accurately interpret the kind of detailed observation that early childhood professionals possess. For example, a parent might comment on how other children's drawings look more sophisticated than those of her child. Rather than going into details of possible developmental delay, the sensitive early childhood practitioner might respond in terms of the factors that influence children's art and focus on the strengths of the child's drawing skills. Another common situation is meeting the parent's request to know who bit her child. Biting is a very difficult behaviour to prevent and staff may or may not know who the offender was. However, it may be in the best interests of all concerned to withhold that information so that children are not labelled and ostracised by other parents and to protect the biter's parents from the possible emotional backlash of the victim's and other children's parents. Reference to a document such as The Australian Early Childhood Association's Code of Ethics (1991) may help provide guidelines for the professional management of information.

One sensitive issue in information sharing is confidentiality. Within a centre meeting, the staff might discuss the progress of a child or problems that a parent has shared about her child. A staff member might be seeking assistance from the group to improve the program designed for the child and such professional discussions are beneficial for the staff members and the child. However, the information and opinions shared at a staff meeting must remain confidential and not be passed on to anyone else, particularly other parents. It is imperative that children and their families are not discussed with anyone outside the centre or in inappropriate venues, such as the supermarket or local shopping centre, because experience has shown that parents usually hear 'on the grapevine' and can justifiably be most upset at this breach of trust. The leader has the responsibility to ensure confidentiality to parents and, by the same token, to staff if for any reason staff performance needs to be discussed. Conflict about inappropriate information management can destroy basic trust between the leader, staff and parents and diminish the quality of the program.

Personality clashes

Conflict between members of early childhood centres has been explained by the use of the term 'personality clash', the implication being that the conflict was inevitable and cannot be resolved because of the fixed nature of the different personalities involved. While psychological research does suggest that personality may be a largely inherited and stable trait (Berk, 1997), individual personality differences are not sufficient to explain why conflict occurs in the first place and is continued by two individuals. The more logical explanation is that the two individuals have chosen not to cooperate and not to meet the needs of the workplace by negotiating a mutually acceptable solution to their differences. In addition, the fact that the conflict is public in nature and is able to continue in the workplace suggests that the psychological climate in the centre accepts and perhaps even subtly encourages conflict as a way of responding to incidents which arise in early childhood settings.

Conflict which is continued by individuals in the workplace can be very destructive to general staff morale and parental confidence in the staff of the centre as well as providing a poor model of human interaction and problem solving for young children. The stereotype of 'personality clash' seems to be used by those who have no intention of working to resolve their differences or to absolve individuals of responsibility for the conflict. The final outcome of the disruption caused to early childhood centres by individuals who choose not to cooperate and get on with the job is that inevitably one of the protagonists does not have a job. This outcome may occur either because one or both staff members choose to resign or because the leader or committee of management decides that the negative effects of continued conflict are affecting the quality of the program and terminate either one or both staff members' employment.

Rigid maintenance of prejudices and stereotyped ideas

Some people, perhaps because of general personality tendencies, rigidly maintain their prejudices and stereotypes even when confronted with contrary evidence. In an area such as early childhood, where the knowledge base and understanding about young children and families is growing and increasing in complexity, staff need to be adaptable and flexible, willing to embrace new ideas and techniques as they become available. Professional relationships which are grounded in communication cannot function properly if some staff members are psychologically bound by outdated assumptions and stereotypes.

Attitudes to children and understanding of appropriate early childhood practice have changed dramatically over time and some attitudes and practices which were once accepted have become outdated, irrelevant and inappropriate for today's society. For example, until the 1960s, physical punishment was believed to enhance obedience. Research now indicates that this is not true (Berk, 1997). In the same way, it used to be thought that tight, authoritarian control over staff members was necessary to ensure that they met their work commitments. However, many researchers have shown that this attitude has a negative effect on many employees' commitment to, motivation for and initiative at work (George & Cole, 1992). Children of single parent families once were considered to be inherently disadvantaged. It is now accepted that the quality of children's experience is dependent upon a range of factors (Hamner & Turner, 1996).

Insensitivity to the need to consider new developments in the early childhood field can promote conflict between staff who want to maintain policy and practice derived from theories and ideas that are now outmoded and those who wish to incorporate current knowledge, understandings and skills into the program. The value of keeping up to date with research findings is explored in Chapter 7.

Resistance to change

The issue of change in the early childhood profession is central to ongoing professionalism and will be discussed in detail in a separate chapter. However, it is important to recognise that employer and employee attitudes to change and subsequent resistance to change can be a source of conflict. Quality early childhood programs are responsive to social, cultural, economic and political changes among others. In the case where either the leader or the staff perceive change as a threat rather than an opportunity for growth, and where energy is misdirected into resisting change rather than anticipating and easing the implementation of change, tension and frustration on the part of those who understand the need to be responsive to change can be a source of conflict.

The effective leader understands that change is threatening for many people and that resistance to change is a normal human response. Nevertheless, the leader has to work to develop positive attitudes to change, in herself and/or staff members and towards overcoming areas of resistance to change in constructive ways rather than permitting any uncertainty about change to escalate into a situation of conflict.

There are many potential sources of conflict in early childhood settings and the preceding discussion has highlighted but a few. The effective early childhood leader will analyse her own setting in order to determine the likely sources of potential conflict and determine whether there are any structural modifications which could reduce the potential for conflict. However, conflict is inevitable and necessary for organisational growth. The next step is to manage conflict constructively.

Typical ways of managing conflict in early childhood centres

There are a number of commonly used approaches to dealing with conflict which vary in their outcome and degree of effectiveness. Unfortunately, the family appears to have been the training ground for many people where, through observation and personal experience, ineffective and even destructive ways of dealing with conflict have been the norm. Unless people are particularly skilled in techniques for conflict management, the methods used by individuals in their personal relationships are usually inappropriate for the professional situation. Therefore, effective leaders will examine their own styles for responding to conflict and evaluate their outcomes in terms of the goals of the centre and staff morale.

The following typical ways of dealing with conflict (Simpson, 1977) can be observed in many early childhood centres but tend to have unproductive or negative outcomes for the leader and the staff.

Denial and withdrawal

One common way of responding to conflict is to deny its existence. For example, the leader announces the new roster. Jane notices that she has another week of early shifts. Her tense body language and tone of voice communicate that she is unhappy with the new roster as she mutters to herself 'How typical! I'm always given the worst shifts. The coordinator must really have it in for me!'. Overhearing this complaint, the coordinator asks Jane if she has a problem with the new roster. Jane is non-assertive about her problem and replies 'No, nothing's wrong. Everything is just fine' and walks away. This form of denial means that, even when an opportunity is presented to bring a potential problem up for discussion, there will be no movement towards acknowledging that there is a difference of opinion, defining what the difference is about or discussing possible alternatives. By denying that a problem exists, Jane has locked herself into a situation that she is unhappy with and she will experience the problems associated with being non-assertive which were discussed in Chapter 2.

In this example, Jane has also walked away. She has withdrawn from the situation and her behaviour indicates that she is not willing to participate in any discussion that may arise out of the posting of the new roster. It is almost impossible to resolve a conflict if one of the parties withdraws by turning silent or by physically removing themselves from the situation. Unless the other person is willing to be assertive and follow up the person who has withdrawn, it is unlikely that the issue will be resolved. The 'silent treatment' is manipulative and destructive to relationships as well as productivity, and the unresolved tension that is sure to build up will probably be released in an explosive outburst where the problem may be exaggerated and other past issues brought up to illustrate the injustice that has been suffered.

Denial and withdrawal do not resolve conflicts but keep the dysfunctional tension buried just beneath the surface. The problem which was initially small is likely to re-emerge later in a different form or as a larger problem for the leader to deal with.

Suppression and smoothing over

In this approach to conflict management, the parties acknowledge that a conflict exists but devalue its importance or significance to them. Using the above example of the new roster, Jane could acknowledge that she was not happy with the shift arrangement but would proceed to suppress her real feelings about the matter saying something like 'Well, I don't really want to do those early shifts again but it doesn't matter. I guess I'm used to them by now.' The leader could attempt to smooth over the problem by commenting 'It all works out in the long run, Jane. We all have to do our share of early shifts. I'll probably be on next time.'

Another way of suppressing and smoothing over conflicts is to minimise the degree of difference between the two parties. Staff members who disagree about a discipline practice might comment, 'I know it's pretty much the same thing but I would have done it differently' or 'Basically we're coming from the same point of view. It's just that I would do it a bit differently.'

The aim of suppression or smoothing over is to move away from the problem as quickly as possible and not to permit any real exploration of the different perspectives. The outcome is that the two parties are no closer to understanding one another's perspective, no closer to negotiating a mutually accepted practice but both are likely to feel that their position is really the right position and will continue with the practice that initiated the feelings of tension. The problem is likely to re-emerge at a later time or in a different form and be more difficult to deal with because people have become entrenched in their positions. An opportunity for gaining a different perspective, learning and professional growth is lost when suppression is used.

Power and dominance

The use of power in conflict situations demonstrates a basic lack of respect for the other parties. Power can be wielded from one's position in the hierarchy, for example, by the leader as the legitimate authority, by the second-in-charge with delegated authority, through group unity with the room staff standing against administration from the perspectives of longevity, seniority or possession of qualifications, or by essential staff such as the cook or cleaner without whom it is impossible to meet minimum standards and requirements. Power can also be exerted by dominating conversations with a loud voice, by interrupting others and not letting them finish what they want to say, by crying and by using intimidating non-verbal communication.

Taking the example of Jane and the new roster, Jane could exert power and dominance over the other members of staff by behaving in an angry and aggressive way, by confronting the leader and demanding that the roster be changed, by pressuring non-assertive staff members to change shifts with her, by interrupting others and refusing to leave the coordinator's office until she got what she wanted or by threatening to take the issue to a higher authority, such as the committee of management or the union. While Jane's behaviour might achieve a change in the roster, it will be at the expense of her respect from and relationships with others as well as lowering the quality of the program while staff deal with other disruptions that such aggressive outbursts bring.

The use of power to force others to submit or give way for peace and harmony can appear to result in the resolution of the problem but creates resentment, anger, bitterness and eventually rebellion or subtler forms of sabotage from members of the group. Power is an aggressive means of responding to conflict and, rather than resolving conflict, power and dominance are more likely to escalate conflict in the long term. While other staff members might accept that one person can achieve their own ends in such a way, eventually they will feel exploited, perceive the leader as weak and possibly interpret the organisational climate as one where power and dominance is accepted as the norm for moving towards one's goals. Instead of resolving one problem by permitting a display of power to be used to achieve certain ends, the leader may find that she has to deal with others who perceive this to be an effective form of conflict resolution.

Constructive approaches to conflict management

There are a number of ways that conflict can be managed in early childhood settings which are more likely to produce positive outcomes for all involved. The basic premise of conflict management is to open and maintain channels of effective communication so that each party perceives herself to be acknowledged and understood. The following three step framework is simple and easy to implement by leaders in early childhood settings.

Assertion

When an incident is perceived as having the potential to develop into a conflict, the first important step is to recognise that it is problem which needs to be responded to. If the leader or any party involved in the incident can make an appropriately assertive statement which describes the behaviour, problem, performance, issue or action and her associated feelings, this signals that one party has a different perception of the incident to that of other people. For example, when Jane had read the new roster, she could have made an assertive statement to the leader such as 'When I saw that I had been rostered on for another week of early shifts, I felt pretty upset because I have just finished doing a week of early shifts. I'd prefer to have a week of late shifts next week.'

The advantages of being assertive in this situation are that Jane has described the specific issue that her concern is related to, has vented her emotional reaction in an appropriate way and has indicated a preference for managing the situation in a way that will meet her needs. Other advantages are that Jane has directed her statement to the appropriate person, the leader who is responsible for the roster, and responded to the situation when it occurred therefore avoiding a build-up of emotional tension and associated apprehension about confronting the leader. She has focused on the issue and not sought to blame or focus on the personality. The use of the 'I' statement indicated that she took responsibility for owning the problem. While being assertive cannot guarantee that Jane will be allocated the shifts that she wants, she has the satisfaction of having attempted to have her needs met in an appropriate manner.

This well-known assertive format:

When (description of the action, issue etc.)............................,
I felt (description of the feeling or emotion)...........................,
because (explanation of importance or relevance)....................
I'd prefer (indication of an alternative) ....

can assist in handling a range of disagreements and differences and prevent them from building up into more major disputes. If the assertion does not achieve the desired outcome, a further assertion can be valuable which lets the other person know that you empathise with their position but still require a modification of the issue. A statement such as 'I can see your point of view but I'd still prefer . . .' can communicate an intention to pursue the matter further. While it may be necessary to repeat the assertion a number of times, there comes a point where it is necessary to recognise that this technique for resolving the issue is not working. A different strategy needs to be selected.

Negotiation

If being assertive does not achieve a satisfactory resolution of the conflict, it is useful to move to a position of negotiation. In this step, the unsatisfactory nature of the situation is highlighted along with the motivation to achieve a mutually acceptable solution to the problem. This is important for situations where the aim is both to achieve goals and to maintain harmonious relationships. It is essential to communicate a cooperative intention, highlighting the costs of continuing the conflict and the benefits of resolving the conflict.

When negotiating a conflict, planning and timing are important. A meeting to discuss the issue needs to be set for a time when both parties are free and there is sufficient time to work through the issue. The first step is to obtain a joint definition of the conflict which is precise and does not exaggerate the problem. Both parties need to be fully aware of and communicate understanding of the other person's perspective and feelings about the conflict. Argumentative approaches and threats should be avoided. Concrete outcomes or alternatives should be emphasised. When moving towards an agreement, it is essential that the agreement be mutually acceptable and not the desired outcome of the dominant party. In situations where there has been difficulty in achieving a negotiated agreement, it can be useful to spell out the agreement in writing detailing the specific nature of the agreement, the ways the two parties will behave differently in the future, the way in which any breach of the agreement will be dealt with and the way in which the two parties can check on how well the agreement is meeting both their needs.

Punctual return from tea break is an example of how a negotiated agreement can work. For example, Susan has been assertive with Pam who consistently returns late from morning tea. She has asserted 'When you return late from morning tea, I feel angry because the children are late in packing up and getting ready for lunch. I'd prefer it if you came back by eleven o'clock.' But this has not resolved the problem. Susan then moves to a position of negotiation saying 'I'm really concerned with how we are coping with the transition from morning routine into lunchtime. I'd like us to discuss it in our planning time on Wednesday.' In the planning session, Susan empathises with Pam's position, for example, 'I know it's a real rush to get to the shop for a morning tea cake. There's no time left to have a cup of coffee. But I'm having trouble coping with all the things that have to be done to get the children and the room ready for lunch when you are not back on time. I can see that my stress is having an effect on our work. If we can sort this out, we'll both be more relaxed for our own lunch and the afternoon with the children. Have you got any ideas about what we might do?'. If a negotiated agreement is reached, Pam will agree to be back at a certain time and will understand the consequences of breaking the agreement. Susan and Pam will also discuss the smooth transition from morning to lunchtime in their planning meetings.

Problem solving

In cases where one party refuses to negotiate an agreement to a conflict or where a negotiated agreement does not work or breaks down, it is essential to move quickly to a problem-solving strategy. It is possible that the three steps, assertion, negotiation and problem solving, are employed in the same interaction. However, a number of attempts at assertion and negotiation are often employed before moving to a problem-solving approach. An assertive communication style is appropriate when using problem-solving strategies where conflicts are defined as mutual problems to be solved.

When employing a problem-solving approach, there are several steps which can be followed:

- Clarify the problem. What is the real issue? Where does each party stand on the issue?
- Gather facts and information if necessary.
- Generate or develop a number of alternatives by brainstorming.
- Evaluate and set priorities for the alternatives in order to determine the best solution. Create solutions by considering all alternatives.
- Plan the means of evaluating the most acceptable solution following a period of implementation.
- If the first solution chosen does not work (which can be a real possibility), return to the first step and begin the process again.

The problem-solving approach incorporates a collaborative perspective on conflicts. If one person has a problem, then we as a group have a problem. Blame is not apportioned. It acknowledges that all parties have the expertise to resolve problems which arise. It emphasises the intention to reach resolution rather than permitting the defense of particular positions. A problem-solving approach is a 'win-win' situation in which everyone's needs are respected and where people are invited to cooperate and contribute to the resolution of the issue. An attitude of 'we can work it out' communicated by the leader to the staff and parents can stimulate new levels of trust, more supportive relationships and greater commitment to the team and the job.

In summary, effective leaders in early childhood settings will place great emphasis on developing their own skills for managing conflict and on teaching the staff to view conflict as normal and as an impetus for personal and professional growth. They will implement recognised management practices for handling disputes and encourage staff to assume responsibility for handling their own problems. In addition, they will encourage a professional climate where colleagues are aware of and understand one another's expertise and where individual differences are valued. The leader will appreciate her ethical responsibility for managing conflicts constructively. She and the staff will be aware of the role of conflict in team development which is discussed in Chapter 5 on Team Building and together will take responsibility for assisting the team's progress to more productive working relationships.

4

Decision making

Decision making is the crux of the leadership process and is the means by which leaders plan, organise and guide members of the early childhood centre towards accomplishing the centre's goals. It is an extremely important skill for early childhood leaders where decisions affect the lives of children, parents, staff, the community and the overall profession. Decision making involves a choice, guided by professional standards, between two or more alternatives and can be regarded as a step in the larger processes of problem solving in goal-directed groups (Robbins, 1996). The quality of the decisions made will impinge upon the quality of the service provided because both the quality of work (i.e. task performance) and the quality of life (i.e. group morale) are affected by this ethical aspect of leadership.

What separates a mediocre leader from an effective leader is usually the quality of her decisions (Varner, 1984). Decisions are effective to the extent that they meet the following criteria:

- the resources of the group are fully utilised;
- time is well-used;
- the decision is correct or of high quality;
- all the required group members fully implement the decision; and
- the problem-solving ability of the group is enhanced.

In organisations which are primarily focused upon meeting the needs of human beings, such as early childhood centres, decisions are a focus of daily activity. While many daily decisions are about trivial things, others involve complex issues, such as programming and curriculum decisions, menu decisions, decisions about what information is publicised in the newsletter, staffing decisions, decisions about parent involvement and financial, policy and ethical decisions. The leader is usually responsible and accountable for the majority of the decisions required for the efficient operation of an early childhood centre but there a variety of ways in which decisions can be made. The decisions may be routine, problem-solving or innovative in nature. The method of decision-making chosen by the leader will be influenced by the nature of the decision to be made, who is included in the decision-making process, the desired quality of the decision, the extent to which those affected by the decision accept it and the level of support given to implementing the decision.

Decision-making style is linked to the personal characteristics and style of the early childhood leader, to the characteristics of the group, the nature of the decision to be made and the context. In recent times, the focus has been upon assisting leaders to make rational, cognitive and objective decisions. The use of sophisticated computer simulations and mathematical models which are based on information management and its systematic analysis are examples of decision-making techniques which have attempted to bypass the human, emotional and subjective element of the decision-making process. However, the human input into decision making cannot be ignored because good decisions often involve a combination of reason and emotion, fact and feeling, objectivity and intuition. Hasenfeld (1983:29) suggests that, in decision making, leaders search '. . . for a satisfying solution by constructing a simplified model of reality that is based on past experiences, selective perception of existing stimuli, and familiar alternatives'. This combination may stimulate the creative aspect of decision making which differentiates good and poor decision makers (Robbins, 1996).

Although many leaders would argue that they use a rational approach to decision making which involves gathering the relevant information and making an informed choice, some problems in early childhood services do not lend themselves easily to rational decision making, for example, behaviour management, ethical dilemmas and staffing decisions. Non-rational factors such as lack of knowledge, time pressures or organisational structure will affect the ability to be rational. Given the degree of influence of subjective values and opinions in the early childhood field, irrationality is likely to impede rational decision making (Neugeboren, 1985). Faulty logic, lack of analytical skills and abilities and permitting emotional issues to cloud the situation can result in poor quality decisions. The Code of Ethics which has been developed by national early childhood professional bodies, among them The Australian Early Childhood Association (1991) was designed as a reference point to assist staff with some of the difficult decisions. To date, early childhood practitioners have not generally recognised its value with regard to decision making (Rodd & Clyde, 1991) and are under-utilising a valuable resource for rational decision making.

Types of decisions

Decisions can be classified into two general categories: programmed decisions and non-programmed decisions. Programmed decisions are appropriate for routine, regularly occurring incidents and previously encountered situations and minimise the need for the decision maker to exercise discretion. In programmed decision making, an approach that has been found to be successful in previous situations is applied. It is very much a case of 'If this happens, do that'. For example, if a parent does not arrive to collect her child on time, the situation calls for a programmed decision because the decision maker will follow policy and do what others would have done in the same situation. All staff in early childhood centres make programmed decisions every day. Pre-service and post-initial training provides early childhood practitioners with a repertoire of programmed responses which can be applied to frequently occurring situations in early childhood centres. Goals and objectives, standards, policies and procedures are tools to guide early childhood leaders in effective programmed decision making.

Non-programmed decision making is used in relatively novel, ambiguous, unstructured and spontaneous situations for which the organisation has not developed policies and procedures. A more general problem-solving approach is required to customise the solution for the specific situation. For example, the selection of an Assistant Coordinator or second-in-charge is a non-programmed decision, as is the development of a program or curriculum. Non-programmed decisions are based on the judgement, intuition and creativity of the leader and consequently necessitate a more competent decision maker. It is more likely that the leader of an early childhood centre will have specific responsibility for making non-programmed decisions. In early childhood services, where administrative responsibility for children, staff and parents is becoming less routine, more ambiguous and less amenable to programmed decisions, leaders will need to gain skills in effective decision making.

Carlisle (1979) suggested a framework which is useful for leaders of early childhood centres. He argues that there are three types of decisions: intuitive, judgemental and problem solving. Intuitive decisions are based on feelings and emotions rather than rationality. Although some objective information is used to guide the decision, hunches, intuition and feelings are uppermost in influencing the leader to 'feel right' about the decision regardless of information or advice to the contrary. Experienced leaders might come to high quality decisions using the intuitive approach but the disadvantages of being swayed by one's ego, lack of perspective and devaluing important information may lead to inappropriate decisions which the leader is unable to explain or defend. Intuitive decision making might be employed in the hiring of a staff member where, qualifications and experience being equal among applicants, the leader simply has 'a gut feeling' that a particular applicant would fit in better with the existing staff team. In dealing with a particularly vulnerable parent, the leader might intuitively feel that sharing information about her child's lack of progress would be detrimental to the parent's well-being and decide to withhold the information for the time being.

Judgemental decisions are based upon expert knowledge and experience where the leader is able to predict accurately the outcome of particular courses of action or decisions. The leader's technical expertise means that little time is needed to reflect upon the decision because the problem has been encountered and successfully handled before. Quick judgements may be accurate but there will always be a situation in which the basic assumptions or underlying conditions have changed and are no longer relevant to the decision. Judgemental decisions might be appropriate for ensuring that the centre complies with the local regulations, which staff will be allocated to a particular group of children or decisions concerning the medical treatment of a child whose parents cannot be contacted.

The problem-solving approach to decision making is useful for situations where more information is needed and where time is required to study, analyse and reflect upon the problem. Preventative decision making is also included under the problem-solving approach where the leader looks ahead and, on the basis of existing information and conditions, anticipates what might occur. However, the quantity of information available to the leader is not the central issue (Varner, 1984). Being flooded with information can delay the problem-solving process. Poor quality or irrelevant information will produce low quality decisions. It may not be the amount of information that is accessed by the leader but how key the information is to the decision to be made. The problem-solving approach is a rational method where systematic, objective steps are undertaken in order to solve complex or previously unencountered problems to which there may be several possible solutions. Problem solving as an approach for decision making would be appropriate for any major change to the centre such as enrolment policy, program management or hours of operation, staff changes or the response to complaints from parents regarding program or curriculum focus.

These three types of decisions highlight another aspect of decision making, that is, the relative effectiveness of the individual versus the group. Both the intuitive and judgemental approaches may be used by individuals and accepted by staff and parents on the basis of the leader's expertise. However, if the decision proves to be inappropriate or poor, the leader is likely to bear the brunt of the group's dissatisfaction, resentment and diminished morale. The problem-solving approach may be undertaken by one individual but, given the nature of the situation and the time required to gather, analyse and evaluate information and develop possible solutions, the sharing of the responsibility for this process among group members is likely to result in higher quality and faster decision making. Early childhood professionals are cautioned about the over-use of intuitive and judgemental approaches to decision making because of certain limitations which are inherent in such approaches. These limitations are discussed in Chapter 7 as part of a fuller discussion about sources of information for decision making. Awareness of the range of available sources of information, other than intuition and judgement, is essential because it provides early childhood practitioners with an opportunity to create a better match between the problem to be solved and the method employed in order to come up with the most appropriate solution.

Methods of decision making

Johnson and Johnson (1996) have outlined a number of methods of decision making which vary according to individual and group input. A review of the literature on group decision making reveals that, in some situations, decisions made by groups can be superior to those made by individuals. However, Robbins (1996) points out that group decisions are rarely better than the best performer in the group; that groups consume more resources so any improved effectiveness in group decision making must be counterbalanced against poorer efficiency; and the type of situation as well as the interpersonal relationships in the group impact on the quality of group decision making. Several decision-making methods which involve individual and group input have been summarised and evaluated.

Individual decision making by the designated leader

This is a method where the leader makes the decision independently of the group. This style may not be the preferred style of the leader but she may be placed in this position because of group apathy or group members' stereotyped beliefs about the degree of expertise, power and responsibility of the leader. Many leaders of early childhood centres have complained that group norms operate where they are expected to make most of the decisions because they are the designated leaders regardless of whether the decision would be better handled by the group. The other staff members do not see it as their role or responsibility to participate in decision making but rely on the leader to perform this role. The disadvantages of this approach are a lack of commitment of the group to the implementation of the decision, possible staff disagreement, resentment and hostility about lack of involvement in the decision-making process and under-utilisation of the resources of the group. It is not uncommon for staff and/or parents to go along with the leader's decisions until the leader makes an unpopular decision which results in overt or subtle conflict between the staff and/or parents and the leader. This method of individual decision making is appropriate in circumstances where the group may lack the skill to make the decision and where there is insufficient time to involve group members.

Individual decision making by the designated expert

This method is similar to that outlined above but where an individual member of the group is acknowledged as having expertise in a particular area and given the authority to make the decision. An example of appropriate use of this method would be delegating the purchase of musical equipment to the staff member who is most qualified and experienced in the music area. The research on decision making supports the notion that high quality expertise can result in high quality decisions by individuals. However, if it is essential for group members to accept the decision, then having group members participate in the decision-making process is logical. Apart from having the advantage of utilising the resources of the group, the advantages and disadvantages of this method are the same as in the previous method described above.

Decision by averaging the opinions of individuals

With this method, group members may be consulted individually or at a meeting to find out what each person thinks. The final decision is based on the most popular choice or alternative identified by the members. For example, determining the most popular topic for the speaker at the Annual General Meeting could be undertaken using this method. The difficulties associated with this approach are the lack of group discussion and interaction, unresolved conflict which may impact on future group decision making and the possibility that non-assertive members will voice what they believe the leader wants to hear or what they believe will obtain personal approval from the leader in a personal, one-to-one interview. However, this approach is useful when an urgent decision has to be made, when it is difficult to get group members together for a meeting (as with shift work and rosters in early childhood centres or distances between staff in different centres), when staff or parent commitment is necessary to effectively implement a decision or when the group lacks the harmony, motivation or skills to make the decision any other way.

Decision by the leader following group discussion

With this method, the group has the opportunity to discuss the situation but the leader reserves the right to make the final decision. In this method, the group is consulted by the leader and has the opportunity to provide input but has no responsibility for the final decision. Consulting with the group about the funding submission or details to be included in the annual report would be appropriate for this method. The level of discussion will be an important factor in this method with the leader needing to employ sophisticated communication skills to ensure that open, honest discussion is facilitated. With this method, there is benefit from group discussion but the disadvantages associated with decisions by averaging individuals' opinions can influence the quality of decision finally taken.

Decision by minority

The decision is delegated by the leader or the group to a small committee comprised of individuals with appropriate knowledge and skills who will consider the issue, take a decision and report back to the larger group. This method can be useful where a routine decision is required, for a problem-solving decision where not everybody needs to be involved in the process or where only a few members have the relevant resources. The organisation of a centre-based in-service program or the end-of-year function could be handled appropriately by a small group of staff and/or parents. The production of a parent handbook also lends itself to this method. Again, because of the lack of involvement of the wider group, the disadvantages inherent in the previous methods of decision making apply to this method.

Decision by majority vote

Following a period of group discussion, a vote is taken either publicly or anonymously, and the alternative favoured by the majority of the group members is accepted. This is a common decision-making method in early childhood centres and has the advantages of permitting group discussion and interaction as well as utilising the resources of the group. Many routine decisions, for example, the purchase of food and cleaning materials, the choice of a particular speaker for an in-service afternoon, and problem-solving decisions, for example, the establishment of dispute and grievance procedures, can be handled by majority vote following discussion. Again, the productivity of the discussion will be dependent on the communication skills of the person chairing or facilitating the discussion. Indeed, the end result could be achieved without full participation of all group members with non-assertive members of the group overpowered by more vocal members. It is also possible to alienate the minority whose needs and interests may be denied in the final decision with the result being lack of commitment to implement the decision. Decision by majority vote can be subject to lobbying by those individuals with vested interests in certain decisions which may not be in the best interest of the group.

Decision by consensus

This method is considered by many to be the most effective means of decision making, producing innovative, creative and high quality decisions. In this method, the issues are thoroughly discussed with each group member participating fully until a basic agreement which is acceptable to everyone involved is reached. The decision has been the responsibility of each member who is then partially accountable for the effective implementation of the decision. The development of a discipline statement, centre goals, centre philosophy and general curriculum issues can be handled using this method. The advantages of the consensus method are that the full resources of the group are utilised, full commitment to the implementation of solutions to serious and complex problems is gained and confidence in future decision making by the group is enhanced. The disadvantages of this method are that it can be very time-consuming for a group to arrive at consensus, it requires a high level of motivation and psychological energy and is inappropriate for any decision which has to be made in a time of emergency, pressure or high stress.

A phenomenon called 'Group Think' (Hampton, Summer & Webber, 1983; Kostelnik, 1984) has been found to affect the quality of decisions made by consensus. Group Think refers to a mode of reasoning that individual group members engage in when their desire for consensus overrides their ability to assess a problem realistically or to consider a wide range of possible alternative courses of action. Critical thinking is sacrificed for consensus and a sense of unanimity. People refrain from offering opinions that do not appear to favour the thinking of the majority of the group and articulate views which are perceived to be in line with the group's direction. The result is a low quality decision which will diminish the group's confidence in its ability to produce innovative, creative, problem-solving decisions. Leaders need to become familiar with the phenomenon of Group Think and take steps to avoid the ramifications of this phenomenon such as adopting an initial stand of impartiality, assigning someone to act as devil's advocate, developing alternative scenarios, re-examining previously discarded alternatives and holding second chance meetings for everyone to express residual doubts and concerns. In this way, decision by consensus is more likely to reflect real consensus rather than the pressures of Group Think.

While the disadvantages of group decision making have been outlined, there are a number of limitations to individual decision making which need to be considered by leaders in early childhood centres. First, some leaders have the tendency to put off decision making until it is too late for effective action. The opportunity is lost or the problem has become so big that it is not easily solved. Secondly, some leaders time decision making so that, while not acting too late, they ensure that no significant progress can be achieved. Equilibrium is maintained and the organisation is kept on track but change and innovation are discouraged. Varner (1984) describes these types of leaders in early childhood centres as 'undertakers' and 'caretakers'. These types of leaders do not demonstrate skill in three important factors related to decision making: judgement, the risk to be taken and the information needed to make better decisions. Varner argues that it is the 'risk taker' (who considers the prevailing circumstances at the time the decision has to be taken, assesses the degree of urgency or the risk factor necessitating the decision and utilises the amount, type and quality of the information available at the time) who will make the most effective decisions. Early childhood leaders need to assess their personal tendencies and gain training and experience in decision making so their judgement, timeliness and skills of critical analysis can be nurtured. Confidence to make decisions and take acceptable risks (skills which research suggests are poorly developed in many women) is enhanced with training. Until a degree of skill is obtained in decision making, early childhood leaders should consider the benefits of the group decision-making process.

Saracho (1988) points out another problem which may affect the quality of decisions that early childhood professionals make, that of field dependent versus field independent cognitive processing styles. Field independent individuals tend to employ their own internal standards and values as sources to guide them in processing information, that is, they can separate and abstract objects from the surrounding field and use analytical skills to solve problems that are presented in reorganised or different contexts. On the other hand, field dependent individuals focus on external points of reference and are dependent on authority as guidelines for information processing. The attributes of field dependence are related to the formation of empathetic relationships with others which is the focus of direct care with children and interaction with parents and staff. However, the more analytical attributes of field independence are related to the cognitive flexibility necessary for quality decision making and problem solving. While most human beings possess some of the characteristics of both styles of information processing, Saracho (1988) suggests that leaders of early childhood services need to develop some of the attributes of field independence to enhance their professional performance which encompasses the leadership role.

Professional ethics and decision making

Leadership involves making decisions which are sound because they are grounded in ethics as well as practice. Being an ethical leader is discussed more fully in Chapter 9. However, the relevance of a code of ethics to guide professional decision making needs to be highlighted for members of those professional groups, such as early childhood practitioners, who have the autonomy to exercise considerable discretion in terms of how they interact with consumers of their service as well as how they operate and conduct their service. A professional code of ethics provides a protocol for critical reflection by practitioners about their practice and relationships, acts as a reference point for professional behaviour and enhances confidence and ability to make appropriate and valid decisions when ethical concerns are present. A code of ethics can provide guiding principles for decision making about obligations and responsibilities in daily practice (Stonehouse & Creaser, 1991), can make decision making easier because it provides a basis for action which is less likely to be challenged by those inside and outside the profession (Feeney & Kipnis, 1991), as well as playing an important role in professionalisation, that is, the establishment and maintenance of standards within a profession (Coady, 1991).

The Australian Early Childhood Association's Code of Ethics provides guidelines concerning what early childhood professionals are committed to provide in terms of quality programs for young children and their parents. While it does not attempt to provide a prescriptive or 'right' answer to the complex questions and ethical dilemmas faced by early childhood practitioners, it does assist with assisting practitioners in working out what is right and good rather than expedient and simply practical and it does point to attitudes and behaviours which practitioners should never engage in or condone (Stonehouse & Creaser, 1991). As such, reference to the Code of Ethics can help expedite both day-to-day and long term decision making regarding what responsible early childhood professionals should and should not do (Rodd & Clyde, 1991).

Guidelines for decision making

Many authors have constructed a set of guidelines which can be used by novice and experienced decision makers alike to improve the quality of their decisions. A set of simple steps such as those indicated below can assist leaders and groups in early childhood centres in the process of decision making.

1   Ascertain the need for a decision by defining the situation, problem or goal. Does an unsatisfactory situation exist? Is there some disparity between what is and what should be? Who is the situation unacceptable for? Is the situation a symptom of another underlying problem? What are the hidden agendas if any? In defining the situation, the effective leader will attempt to gather the facts and feelings as close to the reality of the situation as possible.

2   Establish the decision criteria. Identify the characteristics which appear important in making the decision. Collect and study the relevant opinions, facts and information. Allocate weight to the criteria in order to develop priorities in the decision criteria. Know which criteria are central and which are peripheral to the decision.

3   Develop alternative solutions and formulate choices. It is important to identify all of the different alternatives that are available. Avoid evaluation at this stage. It is the leader's responsibility to explore all existing possibilities to ensure a fair and intelligent decision. Refrain from formulating preferences and expectations as alternatives are uncovered.

4   Evaluate the alternatives in terms of the likely results of choosing that direction. The strengths and limitations of each alternative should be compared with the relative weightings established in Step 2. Questions such as when, where, how, with whom and what are the likely results need to be answered

for each alternative. Feelings about each alternative need to be considered at this stage because they can colour and alter rational reasons for particular alternatives.

5   Select the best alternative. Choose the solution that appears to be the most appropriate and makes the most sense. Avoid procrastinating and postponing the decision. Note that the 'best' alternative at the time is still a subjective choice and might turn out to be inappropriate later. Despite the systematic and objective efforts of the leader and group, a wrong choice can be made.

6   Follow through to support the implementation of the decision. Provide personal support to those who will implement and maintain the decision. Stimulate interest and enthusiasm in the process, ensure backup and sufficient time for implementation and communicate shared responsibility and accountability for the success of the decision.

7   Evaluate the effectiveness of the decision in resolving the initial problem. Be flexible and keep an open mind in case the first choice was inappropriate. Be willing to modify the initial decision or engage in the decision-making process again utilising the present information to reach a new alternative.

In the more general process of problem solving, the same steps are employed. Problem solving (as opposed to decision making) is useful when an element of conflict exists in the situation. The situation can be defined as a mutual problem to be solved rather than a win-lose situation. Because conflict triggers emotional responses, it is important to channel the emotional energy towards constructive ends by adopting appropriate win-win attitudes. In problem solving, it is beneficial if the participants focus on the positive results associated with the process of arriving at a solution. The group members need to have developed a certain attitude to conflict, so that it is regarded as a healthy and normal part of group process, and be willing to communicate honestly and openly with each other concerning the issue. Conflict management is discussed in detail in Chapter 3.

In summary, the challenge of leadership is for the early childhood professional to develop her vision and assertiveness in order to make effective and ethical decisions which will move the organisation towards achieving its goals while maintaining a sense of cooperation, loyalty and harmony in group members. The leader should focus attention on the big picture and not become pre-occupied with day-to-day details. Skill needs to be developed in non-programmed decision making where judgement, intuition and calculated risk taking produce creative approaches by the leader to goal attainment and to the situations and problems which emerge in any centre.

5

Building and leading a team

In the administration of early childhood centres, considerable emphasis has been placed upon the significance of effective leadership. The style of leadership exercised in early childhood centres has been found to set the standards and expectations for the other staff to follow (Powell & Stremmel, 1987). Yet, numerous studies of work groups suggest that in groups that are successful in meeting the demands of goal attainment and harmonious relationships, the burdens of leadership are not placed upon one person but are shared widely (Likert, 1961). In fact, in any human service organisation, all members of staff contribute to the operation and administration of the service, for example, by answering the telephone, dealing with inquiries, making programmed decisions, managing their own problems and responding to the needs of any situation which may arise. Teamwork, in which individual interests and needs are subordinated in order to engage in joint, coordinated activity to achieve the common goals and purposes of a united group, is equally important, particularly in early childhood services which involve people, their relationships and feelings.

Effective leadership and teamwork can have a major impact on the quality of the service offered. Considerable research evidence is accumulating which reveals a connection between young children's development and the stability of care in early childhood settings. Instability of care, be it a result of frequent changes in an early childhood setting or frequent changes of staff within the setting, can have negative effects on children's development

(Hennessey et al., 1992). The tone of the working environment can produce a lack of responsiveness and sensitivity among some staff which can lead to high staff turnover. Effective leadership and teamwork are considered to be factors which contribute to increased self-esteem, job satisfaction and staff morale, reduced stress and a decreased likelihood of staff burnout (Schiller, 1987). The end product of teamwork is an improvement in the quality of care and education for children.

While some people still enter the field with the assumption that the focus of the job is on autonomous work with children, the reality of early childhood centres today is that the work of the early childhood practitioner requires effective interaction with other adults as members of a team (Stonehouse & Woodrow, 1992). When early childhood professionals talk about the staff at their centre, the word 'team' is often used. It is apparent that the concept of teamwork is perceived by current leaders as important for the working conditions of early childhood centres. What constitutes a team can vary from centre to centre. In pre-schools, the team may consist of two adults, the Director and the Assistant. In long day or occasional child-care centres, the team may consist of the entire staff group or of the staff who work together in a room or with a particular group of children. In family day care, the team may mean the coordinator, field workers, office staff and a large group of independent providers who are physically isolated from the centralised administration. Depending on the meaning given to the concept of team, parents may or may not be included in the broader definition. Regardless of its definition, the essence of a team is that all participants work together effectively to achieve a common goal.

Why is teamwork considered to be an important issue in the leadership of early childhood services? Neugebauer (1984b) reports the view of Drucker (1973), a noted management consultant, which is that the team concept of management is ideally suited to organisations that deal in ideas, concepts and services. Early childhood services clearly can be categorised as such organisations. Team management is also related to the current belief in the value of participatory management. It can provide social support to team members which acts to ameliorate the strain, stress and tension present in day-to-day activities in early childhood services and which ultimately can lead to burnout. Interpersonal relationships can become a source of support, satisfaction and stimulation thereby enhancing general group morale. By utilising the unique expertise and resources that each member contributes to the team, motivation and job satisfaction are enhanced which will result in effective accomplishment of the task.

While Australian early childhood professionals recognise certain advantages of teamwork, they have provided anecdotal evidence (Rodd, 1992) which supports Neugebauer's (1984a) assertion that members of early childhood services (the staff and the leader) too often assume that it is the leader's job to keep the team on track, to make decisions and to solve problems. Although all team members may want the team to perform well, when it functions poorly the staff are unlikely to take responsibility. The leader and the staff alike tend to blame the leader for the performance of the entire team. Apparently, early childhood professionals have not yet fully understood the notion of teamwork and how it can be applied in their centres.

What do early childhood professionals understand about teamwork?

Qualitative data from unpublished research (Rodd, 1992) has clarified child-care and family day care coordinators' understanding of teamwork in early childhood services. The data were collected from approximately twenty in-service training programs conducted throughout Victoria during the early 1990s in which nearly 500 participants were asked to respond to four issues. The responses, along with more recent data collected in Britain, have been used to construct a profile of early childhood professionals' perceptions of several pertinent aspects of teamwork.

Firstly, the participants defined their understanding of the term 'team' in early childhood services. This can be summarised as 'a group of people cooperating with each other to work towards achieving an agreed set of aims, objectives or goals while simultaneously considering the personal needs and interests of individuals'. The concepts which were reiterated by each group were: the pursuit of a common philosophy, ideals and values; commitment to working through the issues; shared responsibility; open and honest communication and access to a support system.

The perceived advantages of teamwork were explored in the question 'Why do we work in teams in early childhood services?'. The following advantages were consistently identified:

- support and stimulation;
- a sense of belonging and equality;
- opportunity for growth and development;
- stress reduction;
- facilitation of a pleasant working environment;
- opportunity to work through issues and minimise conflicts;
- the provision of a role model for children and parents;
- an opportunity for staff members to assume a leadership role in the short term;
- assistance for efficiently achieving the same goals;
- shared workload;
- shared human resources and ideas;
- acknowledgement of staff members' professional capacities; and
- increased motivation and commitment to the task or decision.

The participants clearly were aware of the two essential aspects for teamwork: task performance and group relationships. Certain disadvantages to what was termed the 'autocratic delegation leadership style' were highlighted in the responses, among them competition, lack of respect, resentment, isolation and reduced commitment. These factors were considered to reduce the early childhood staff members' ability to get the job done and maintain positive relationships at work.

Although perceptions about the value of teamwork are of interest, it is important to know how closely these perceptions were reflected in expectations about teamwork and in actual experience of teamwork. Participants were asked to identify what they expected when they were involved in teamwork. Expectations regarding participation in an early childhood team can be summarised as:

- all members should pull their weight equally;
- open communication;
- respect for and valuing of each member by each other;
- understanding the roles and responsibilities of other staff members;
- flexibility;
- democratic leadership style from the leader;
- aware of and in tune with others' expectations, needs, interests and goals;
- appreciation of others' skills;
- sharing of roles and responsibilities;

- feelings of satisfaction from working in a team; and
- members accepting and abiding by the group's decision.

Whereas the participants were able to identify generally positive expectations regarding teamwork, their previous experience working in teams had not always been consistent with their expectations. Teamwork in practice appears to be quite a different proposition from teamwork in theory. In relating their previous involvement in teamwork in early childhood centres, the following negative experiences were reported:

- individuals pursuing personal goals rather than centre goals;
- individuals actively or covertly sabotaging the team's work;
- uncertainty about the roles and responsibilities of the leader and the group members;
- authoritarian leadership style of the designated leader;
- lack of respect for each other;
- fragmentation of work;
- isolation of staff members;
- low morale; and
- unresolved conflict which tends to focus on personalities rather than issues.

It appears that although early childhood professionals in Australia and Britain value the teamwork approach to the administration of a centre, some problems exist in galvanising groups of individual staff members into team members (that is, team building) and maintaining team spirit once it has been established. Leadership style was perceived as having a major impact on the development of a team approach in early childhood centres. The designated leader was considered to hold the following roles and responsibilities in relation to the early childhood team:

- overall coordination of the centre;
- the provision of support and guidance;
- the facilitation of open communication;
- the provision of feedback and encouragement;
- the identification of problems and sources of stress;
- to be objective and consistent;
- to be fair;
- to be flexible;
- to know the difference between delegation and 'palming off' different responsibilities;

- the setting and communication of the parameters that the team has to work within;
- the sharing of information;
- to act as a resource and to refer when necessary;
- to act as a buffer between staff and parents;
- to ensure confidentiality;
- the facilitation of group cohesion;
- the encouragement of professional growth and development in all team members;
- to be aware of own limitations;
- to facilitate the meeting of individual, personal needs as well as group needs;
- to be prepared to take control if necessary;
- the acceptance of final responsibility for the team's efforts; and
- to liaise with the outside community.

Team members were considered to hold particular roles and responsibilities in relation to the team's viability and the achievement of its goals. These are summarised below as:

- to keep the lines of communication open;
- to be cooperative and committed;
- for all members to be available to one another;
- to be aware of one's own responsibilities;
- to ensure confidentiality;
- to respect and be tolerant of individual differences;
- to demonstrate respect for the ideology of the team and team effort;
- to accept and acknowledge own and others' limitations;
- to share the workload and expertise;
- to be flexible and to give and take;
- to be reliable and to follow through;
- to develop individual strengths and work on overcoming limitations; and
- to be sensitive to the nature and scope of work relationships.

These data indicate that many early childhood professionals understand that teamwork is more than just turning up for work each day. It involves a special conceptualisation of the roles and responsibilities of both the leader and each team member. For leaders, teamwork means acting more as a facilitator than a superior. For staff members, it means taking an active role in the work situation rather than being a passive follower of instructions and directions. Benefits from teamwork are perceived as accruing for both leader and team members. The inconsistency between expectations and reality in teamwork suggests that early childhood leaders have not developed skill in building and leading teams. An exploration of the stages of team development and team leadership can clarify some of the issues relevant to effective teamwork.

The stages of team development

Team development is not an easy task. It requires concerted, ongoing effort on behalf of each member and an even greater effort from the leader who is ultimately responsible for the process of moving the team from birth to maturity. A number of writers have identified sequences of team development that a group of co-workers will move through over differing periods of time (Adair, 1986; Woodcock, 1979; Woodcock & Francis, 1981). The speed with which each group will accomplish the demands of a particular stage and move on to the next stage is considered to be related to the skill possessed by the leader. Consequently, leaders in early childhood centres need to be informed about the stage of team development at which the group currently functions and possess the skills to assist the group to move as quickly as possible to a higher stage of development (Walker, 1995).

In many ways, the stages of team development are similar to those commonly described for general group development—forming, storming, norming, performing and adjourning (Curran, 1989). The following stages are outlined in terms of the task and relationship requirements for early childhood centres.

Stage 1 Getting together as a team

The first stage in the development of a team is when a group of people become aware that they are going to be working together. This may be when a new centre is established and a completely new group of staff are employed to work together in the centre. More likely, a new person or persons will join an existing group of staff or a person may resign and not be replaced as long as this does not violate the staff:child ratio. Whenever there is a different group composition, the start of a new team has been signalled. This will require assimilation of the new person into the team and accommodation by the existing staff to the new conditions. The leader must address the demands of the task and relationships in order to assist staff to be productive and feel comfortable in this initial stage of team development.

In terms of the task, the major concern is with orientation to the work where structured activities such as information sharing, organising roles and responsibilities and goal setting are important because they act to alleviate staff members' apprehension about change and anxiety about competence to undertake the job. Staff will focus on the designated figure of authority to provide a blueprint for the direction of the centre and may ask a variety of questions, for example 'What are we supposed to do?', 'What happens next?', and 'What are our goals?'. Conformity to the leader's approach will be high and few challenges can be expected. The leader needs to provide clear directions and guidelines for staff at this point which will communicate her vision and values, general objectives and expectations about staff participation and confidence in the team which should result in staff commitment to the centre's program. Staff should be encouraged to set personal goals as a means of ongoing self-evaluation.

The relationship and group morale aspect can be difficult to manage at this initial stage because staff are concerned about belonging, inclusion and rejection and may be unwilling to disclose their personal concerns and weaknesses. They are likely to be concerned with self-protection in what is perceived as an unknown situation so may keep feelings hidden, display little concern for others and be unlikely to listen effectively because their own needs will dominate their attention. The climate of the centre may be characterised by politeness and a wish to avoid contentious issues or anything that might result in conflict. Woodcock and Francis (1981) call this 'ritual sniffing' because the staff are focused upon getting acquainted with the others in the group, assessing others' strengths and weaknesses and generally testing out the situation in order to determine the written and unwritten ground rules which operate in the group. The leader needs to provide opportunities for staff to get to know one another professionally and personally. Introducing some kind of informal social function such as coffee after work or a shared meal before a staff meeting can help facilitate understanding of and acceptance of others in the group and the formation of initial relationships. The leader needs to be available and accessible, non-threatening and observant of the interaction patterns and styles.

When the group members feel moderately comfortable with one another because a degree of trust and security in the people and the task has been achieved, a degree of risk taking in terms of challenging aspects of the task and the expertise of others to undertake the task may emerge. Small indications of conflict may be noticed. The group is now in transition to the next stage of team development.

Stage 2 Confronting conflict in the team

It generally comes as some surprise both to the leader and the team members when the group which initially appeared to get along so well disintegrates into one which is marked by open and covert displays of antagonism to one another, dispute, dissension and discord. In terms of team development, the honeymoon period is over. The challenges for the team members at this second stage are establishing a niche in the pecking order and negotiation of roles and responsibilities. The direction and activities of the leader are likely to be evaluated and possibly challenged by team members who are feeling more confident about their position in the group.

With regard to the task performance aspect of the team, staff become concerned with aspects of the administrative organisation of the centre. Rules, procedures, policies and agendas become the focus of attention with queries about who has the power to direct, control and change the administrative structure. Commitment to the group goals may appear to be reduced as staff debate the overall program. As group members get to know each other better, they also can identify one another's strengths and limitations. This can bring about confrontation regarding values, beliefs and appropriate practice which can produce an organisational climate that is characterised by criticism. Questions and statements such as 'What authority have you got to make that decision?', 'Who makes the rules here, the staff or the Coordinator?', 'Who are you to tell me what to do? I only take directions from the Coordinator!', 'How is my performance going to be appraised?', and 'The Committee of Management can't tell us to do that!' will be heard from staff as they attempt to clarify where the power lies in the centre.

In this second stage, relationships between members of the team become more significant and can be influential in the way in which emerging group differences are dealt with. Staff needs for recognition of their unique contribution to the centre can be met only in an atmosphere of mutual support and respect. These individual needs and subsequently overall group morale can be undermined by a climate which is marked by criticism in an early childhood centre. In order to bolster self-esteem, staff may form cliques and alliances to pressure the leader and other staff members to meet their demands. Increased stress is likely to be experienced by all those connected with the centre, including children and parents, if the in-fighting, power struggles, disputes and destructive criticism are not managed appropriately.

The leader of an early childhood centre needs to have a thorough understanding of conflict and its role in organisations. This has been addressed in Chapter 3. In the process of galvanising a group of disparate individuals into a cohesive team, conflict is inevitable, normal and healthy. It is a sign that the group is growing. The constructive resolution of differences can clear the way for more cooperative and productive endeavour on the part of the team. Ignoring or avoiding conflict in this stage will hinder the team's progress to a more advanced and harmonious stage of development. In groups where conflict and confrontation are not resolved, decision making and problem solving ability is poor, commitment is low and the group members do not enjoy being part of the group. Psychological and/or physical withdrawal may occur which will diminish the team's productivity.

The effective leader whose team is in this second stage of development will need to employ sophisticated communication skills to manage the conflict in order to move people towards greater acceptance, increased trust and commitment to the task. Active listening, assertion and conflict management skills are essential and the leader may need to provide guidelines for handling differences between staff in a professional manner. In addition, the leader needs to be confident in her own ability to manage the situation constructively and communicate confidence in the staff regarding their ability to clarify any issues of concern while maintaining respect for others in the group. Holding individual, small and large group meetings where information, standards and expectations are clarified, and established goals are focused upon, can be useful at this point.

Many leaders of early childhood centres have reported that their team appears 'stuck' in a cycle of conflict which produces high levels of stress for all involved, decreased morale and commitment and high staff turnover. As well as the extra energy required to work in a conflict-prone environment and to attempt to work the problems through, staff resignation and staff replacements are changes which will have to be responded to by the leader and the group. The leader will need to facilitate a sense of closure and re-orient the team to the fact that a new team will be forming. The team will return to the first stage of team development and begin the process of getting together as a team again. If the leader does not possess the confidence and skills to deal with conflict, the same scenario will probably be repeated when the new team moves into the second stage of confronting conflict. Without competent intervention, the cycle is repeated with the resultant perception that the team is conflict prone or 'stuck' in a destructive cycle of discord.

A major disadvantage of extended periods in the second stage is that early childhood centres which experience high staff turnover as a result of unresolved conflict do not capitalise on the training and experience that staff members have gained while working in the centre. The level of service quality that is expected by staff and parents is more difficult to achieve with a high staff turnover. Individual staff gain expertise over time that is not easy to replace. This will place an added burden on the leader because she will be continually involved in staff orientation, initiation and supervision until the new staff attain competence levels to work more independently. The leader will have less time to devote to other important aspects of administering a high quality service. In addition, continuous staff turnover keeps the level of team development at lower levels which requires more input from the leader to ensure that the team advances in its growth.

If the leader manages the challenges of this second stage, the team will begin to resolve personal animosities and to focus back on improving activities and performance related to achieving the centre's goals. The team is advancing to the third stage.

Stage 3 Consensus and cooperation in the team

The assumption that a group which starts to evidence consensus and cooperation is now working as a team is generally accurate. While the group may appear to be operating in a more dynamic manner, members are not yet performing in a unified or methodical way. However, having worked through some of the important issues in the previous stage, the team is now willing to take some risks and experiment with new practices, debate values and assumptions, review methods of operation and discuss issues of management and leadership (Woodcock & Francis, 1981). New confidence gained from resolving the earlier conflicts produces a receptiveness in team members to new ideas and risk taking. If a leader has skilfully handled the first two stages, the team will move quickly through this third stage.

The challenges surrounding task performance issues focus on information sharing, win-win attitudes to problem solving and a willingness to take calculated risks and change. These task-related activities are anchored in the new level of trust that has developed through the management of conflict. Individuals trust both themselves in the job and the other group members. This may motivate previously inactive members of staff to become more involved with a broader range of responsibilities in the centre. Change has begun. A breach of trust at this stage will reverse the team's progress and it is possible that the team will regress to the previous stage. Skill in decision making and problem solving is needed by the leader and by team members in order to capitalise on the team's potential at this point. The leadership style exhibited by the designated leader is important. The group is interested in contribution and participation at this stage, therefore the participatory, democratic style is appropriate for meeting staff members' needs. Some members of the team will be interested in sharing responsibility with the leader so effective delegation will become an important skill in the leader.

The focus of the team at the third stage of development continues to be on group relationships. Having been fragmented by conflict, the staff members now are interested in achieving cohesion. The beginning of a 'team spirit' becomes evident with staff spontaneously referring to themselves and their colleagues as 'the team'. Team members are more open-minded, more willing to listen to and support one another, and able to focus on the needs of the group rather than their own needs. Mutually accepted group norms begin to guide the work and relationships in the centre. The word 'we' is heard more often than 'I' or 'you' when the activities of the centre are discussed. The climate of the centre includes a light-hearted aspect where joking and humour illustrate good-natured attitudes in the staff.

Although conflict and disagreements may still occur, they are perceived as less threatening by the staff and handled differently. The problem-solving approach to conflict and decision making is evident because the team wishes to protect group cohesion and positive relationships.

At this third stage, the role of the leader is to promote consensus and cooperation. Staff involvement and participation in goal setting, the development of polices and their implementation in practice needs to be supported by the leader. A willingness to identify and address potential problems is essential. Open communication, constructive feedback and acknowledgement of contribution to the group will facilitate consensus and cooperation in the team. As the group begins to take pride in its achievements, the group is truly becoming a team and is advancing into the fourth stage.

Stage 4   Effective team performance

The rate at which a group of individuals will proceed to this fourth stage depends on the effectiveness of the leader in facilitating the transition through the previous stages. It is not until this fourth stage that the group of individuals who committed themselves to working together in the first stage can be said to be operating as an effective team.

At this stage, all members of the team are making a unique but equal contribution to the task. The team shares responsibility for the efficient operation of a quality service with the leader. Leadership style is decided according to the situation. Regular review and evaluation of centre goals, policies and practice is undertaken with a view to constant improvement of the service. Staff appraisal, either with the leader or by self-appraisal, is accepted as a means of professional staff development. The team adopts a creative problem-solving approach to its operation and engages in preventive decision making. Change is anticipated, planned for and the team is prepared for and included in phased implementation. The team rewards its performance by articulating a sense of pride concerning its achievements.

The relationship aspect of the team is based on mutual respect and support. Team members recognise their interdependence as well as their independence. Individual differences and successes are valued. People are now able to 'agree to disagree' if mutually acceptable solutions to problems are not forthcoming. The climate is marked by concern for other team members, warmth and friendliness.

The team is working efficiently and members are enjoying their work. The leader is able to relax and enjoy the fruits of previous efforts. However, the leader needs to keep close contact with the various teams in the centre and ensure that any small quality control adjustments are made and shared. Opportunities for contact and relationships with outside groups are pursued and assistance from outside sources is welcomed by team members. The team is willing to extend its energies beyond the confines of the centre. The leader has an opportunity to facilitate the development of appropriate staff members through the mentoring process thereby contributing to the development of another future leader.

A team which reaches this stage of mature development can operate productively for a long period of time as long as attention is given to ensuring effective working methods and the maintenance of relationships. While self-evaluation should be encouraged in all staff members from the time they join the group, formal evaluation of the team and its performance needs to be introduced at this point. This will ensure that questions such as 'How are we going?', 'Where do we want to go next?' and 'What are our needs now?' must be addressed in order to keep the team at its maximum operational efficiency. However, if any of the conditions change, such as a staff member leaving or the dissolution of the group because its purpose no longer exists, the team enters the final stage in its development, that of separation and closure.

Stage 5 Separation and closure

This final stage tends to be ignored by many team leaders who, in their haste to move the team back to a more productive and positive stage, fail to acknowledge the team's need to celebrate or mourn its existence and track record. A change in or the disbanding of a team can occur at any stage in a team's development. The sensitive leader will ensure that the team has an opportunity to experience some form of closure so that staff members can deal with unfinished business which might prevent them from approaching their future working situation positively.

When a team ceases to be operational, the members have to come to terms with two issues: disengagement from the task and separation from and/or closure of relationships. Usually there is a period of time for the team to work these issues through. It is the leader's responsibility to ensure that the team has access to a means of debriefing and bringing closure to the experience. Comments such as 'Remember when Jenny was here? She would have known what to do' or 'Didn't we work well together before all the changes!' suggest that the staff have not had sufficient time to come to terms with the demise of the previous team. These nostalgic memories may interfere with commitment to the new team and acceptance of any new staff members.

If the team has worked well and it has been a satisfying experience for those involved, the staff will be able to celebrate the end of the team by reviewing and evaluating individual development, task performance and work relationships. The team should recognise its accomplishments and express its satisfaction with the process. The emotional responses of the team members to the closure of the group need to be acknowledged and dealt with. Some frustration and anger may be expressed to the leader who will understand that this is part of the normal process of separation. There may also be some confusion about emotional responses with individuals vacillating between feeling happy and satisfied about the team's achievements and sad and angry about the team's break-up. The stress associated with the closure of the team may produce lower quality performance. However, the leader needs to de-emphasise task-related aspects at this point and focus upon meeting the staff members' social and emotional needs in preparation for establishing a new team.

If the ending of the team is marked by a lack of achievement and/or poor relationships, it is more difficult, but even more important, to engage in a process of closure. Each team member's contribution should be reviewed and evaluated as well as the overall group dynamic in order to identify the problems which prevented the team from operating effectively. In this way, the leader and the group members should gain a basis for planning for the next team experience.

Team leadership

Becoming an effective leader in early childhood has an inherent difficulty which few leaders in other professions have to deal with. In some services, for example long-day care, the leader has to adapt on a daily basis to moving from the position of administrative leader to being a member of a room team responsible for direct care of children. The way in which the leader's time has been allocated officially to combine administration and direct care has ensured that both the leader and the team members have to adapt to the constant changes in the leader's position in the team. This can place a great strain on the resources of the leader who is required to relinquish the authority of leadership when working as an equal member of a direct care team and to resume and command that same authority when she is undertaking the administrative functions. Team members can become confused about the appropriate way to interact with the leader when she is in the direct care team role. This constant fluctuation between leader and team member requires sensitive management by the leader. Team leadership has some advantages for early childhood leaders who find themselves in this position.

To review the leader's role in relation to the team, the key functions are to provide and communicate a vision to the group, develop the team culture, set goals, monitor and communicate the team's achievements to the team and relevant others, and to facilitate and encourage the development of individuals. These functions can be fulfilled using the various styles of leadership which have been outlined in Chapter 1. However, in order to engage in the process of 'team leadership' where special effort is devoted to enhancing the team culture in order to achieve better results, the leader also needs to exhibit the following features which differentiate team leadership from other styles of leadership.

An effective team leader:

- uses her personality to lead by example thereby stimulating a particular team culture;
- is innovative and is perceived to be making things better by improving team morale and productivity;
- ensures that constructive relationships are established and maintained with the staff and peers;
- focuses attention on behaviour or the situation not on the person;
- fosters the self-esteem and confidence of team members; and
- coaches team members to improve their performance.

Certain values and approaches have been found to be associated with developing this team leadership orientation. They can assist in matching the leadership style to follower needs and situational demands. Early childhood practitioners will find that developing the following features may be useful in meeting the demands of team leadership.

- Adaptability (the capacity to be responsive and innovative);
- Energetic (action-oriented and committed to work);
- People-oriented (values people and communicates openly);
- Quality consciousness (pays attention to standards of excellence and consumer needs and expectations);
- United (clarifies the common purpose and promotes the value of cooperation);
- Entrepreneurial (autonomous and able to articulate the uniqueness of the service);

- Focused (self-disciplined and predictable); and
- Informal (a relaxed, straightforward approach to people and situations).

These features, values and approaches of team leadership are fundamental to the early childhood leader making things happen in the centre in ways which can increase staff and parent participation. When attempting to build and lead a team, the leader needs to be conscious of the positive impact that team leadership can have on a group of individuals who are working together and incorporate appropriate aspects of the team leadership approach into her style. In addition to the leader's individual style, a systematic, step-by-step approach to team building and maintenance can be followed to assist the team's advancement in productivity.

A framework for team building

As has been discussed previously in the stages of team development, the process of galvanising a group of individuals into a cohesive team is not a quick and painless one. Becoming a team demands effort from every member of the group and requires that the leader relate to the group in a certain way. However, as Neugebauer (1984b) states, developing a group of individuals into a staff team can be a very rewarding experience for a leader. Although numerous obstacles to team building exist in early childhood settings, such as heterogeneous skills, interests and values and the fragmentation of staff through the physical setting and shift work, the process can be implemented gradually with staff encouraged to provide feedback about their satisfaction or otherwise with the process.

The team building process basically focuses on the two dimensions of any team: staff morale and task demands. In order to build team morale, the group needs to be able to provide social support for the interpersonal demands that evolve in any work group. This support may consist of emotional, informational, instrumental or appraisal support. The leader may need to help the group identify how members may be able to assist and support one another. The accomplishment of the task requires an analysis of work demands and the development of role profiles based on the expectations of the leader and peers. The leader will need to respond to the staff's increasing participation in decision making

114

and increasing personal control over how the job is performed. Attention to these two dimensions will produce a cohesive group that works to accomplish specific tasks in a supportive environment (Benton & Halloran, 1991).

Neugebauer (1984b) has devised a specific framework for team building in early childhood settings which is helpful for leaders who want to encourage a team approach in their centres. The five steps outlined in the framework are:

1   Set achievable goals which have been mutually agreed upon by members of the team. Ensure that the assertive staff members do not dominate the process especially during discussion at staff meetings.
2   Clarify roles. Team members work most effectively when their roles are clear to all and free of conflict. Each staff member should be aware of who is responsible for what. While it will be easier to clarify the formal roles that need to be fulfilled, the informal roles which relate to the internal functioning of the group should not be forgotten (Neugebauer, 1984a; Johnson & Johnson, 1996). The leader needs to analyse the group to make sure that someone is taking responsibility for the team task roles (initiating, information gathering, opinion seeking and giving, clarifying, elaborating, energizing, summarising and consensus testing) and team maintenance roles (encouraging, harmonising, compromising, gatekeeping, observing and standard setting).
3   Build supportive relationships, that is build in opportunities for feedback, develop trust and provide resources to stimulate a cooperative team spirit. Teams where members feel supported are more likely to deal with common team problems such as role ambiguity, role conflict and group conflict.
4   Encourage active participation which capitalises on the knowledge and skills of individual team members. In an atmosphere of acceptance, team members will be encouraged to contribute their ideas, opinions and energies. Being part of a cooperative venture can be extremely motivating for team members and this will increase productivity.
5   Monitor team effectiveness. There is little point in putting time and energy into team leadership and the team building process if the team is not achieving the goals effectively or if the team is unhappy with the process. Regular opportunities need to be provided by the leader to assess the extent of goal achievement and how well members are working together as a team. This

review process can help identify any problems and establish their cause as well as assisting with future planning.

The success of the team approach relies on open communication, democratic organisation and effective problem-solving skills. An effective team should fulfil staff needs for participation and support and result in efficient and effective approaches to the task.

Supervision and team performance

The quality of early childhood programs is directly related to the quality of the personnel who operate the program, from the designated leader to the staff who work with children, whether they are trained or untrained, experienced or inexperienced. Given the financial constraints that early childhood services operate under and the likelihood of the continuation of these circumstances, the low salaries for child-care personnel and staff turnover and shortages, the early childhood leader faces an ignominious situation. How can the leader fulfil the staff supervisory responsibilities in ways which maintain staff morale and achieve the goals of the centre? Kolb (1989) suggests that one of the most effective ways of fulfilling the leadership role in early childhood settings is through the supervision of staff. The supervisory techniques employed by leaders can '. . . promote positive relationships . . . among the staff' which will result in '. . . confident, motivated caregivers who want to provide quality care and early education for young children' (Kolb, 1989:16).

Supervision is a professional responsibility of the early childhood leader in which the leader helps staff members to use their knowledge and skills effectively in the performance of their work and to deepen their understanding of professional philosophies and values. However, for leaders of early childhood centres the range of supervisory responsibilities are more complex than just working with staff. In addition, some leaders are required to engage in supervision when they are in the early stages of professional development and themselves in need of supervisory support. To date, early childhood personnel already have assumed a large proportion of the responsibility for supervising the training of future early childhood professionals in student practicum and are responsible for guiding untrained staff in the philosophy and practices of the early childhood profession. Those who are presently engaged in supervision at these levels usually have had little or no training and have limited access to support and backup if problems arise during the process. The process of providing feedback to trained and untrained staff is also part of existing supervisory responsibilities. In addition, with the introduction of voluntary accreditation of early childhood centres in Australia and similar processes in other countries, leaders of early childhood centres will assume greater responsibility for on-the-job training, development and supervision of their staff as well as greater input into the support and education of parents in their parenting role. It is evident that the supervisory responsibility is growing.

Perceptive leaders in early childhood will need to reflect upon their attitudes to and capabilities for the supervisory responsibility. Many people regard the process of supervision with suspicion. This can be an obstacle for those leaders who are responsible for quality early childhood programs. Reluctance by either leader or staff members to participate in a supervision program may reflect the traditional view of supervision which related to control and surveillance. Today, supervision is viewed more commonly as a form of continuing staff development in which staff competence is the overriding objective. Given the increasing participation of staff in the operation and administration of early childhood centres, supervision is no longer considered to be the sole responsibility of one individual, that is, the leader, but more appropriately is regarded as a two-way process between leader and staff member. Moreover, supervision can be conducted formally and informally and on a group or team basis as well as on the traditional one-to-one basis. Supervision can be the means of communicating to staff that they are important assets to the program and that they are valued for their special contribution.

Caruso (1991) points out that the diversity of policies and programs within the early childhood field make the creation of a supervisory profile for early childhood professionals difficult. However, he considers that training and experience are important variables in improving this aspect of professional practice. The following characteristics which are suggested to be appropriate for an effective supervisor in early childhood centres must not be regarded as prescriptive but as providing direction for further professional development:

- expertise in the knowledge and skills and possession of professional values and attitudes relevant for the early childhood profession;

- the ability to transmit knowledge and skills in a manner conducive to adult learning;
- sophisticated communication skills which include listening skills, response skills for appropriate feedback (especially showing appreciation and giving recognition), conflict resolution skills and decision-making skills;
- the ability to anticipate and prepare staff for impending change;
- the ability to involve staff in setting team and individual objectives for short and long term achievement;
- the ability to monitor progress on a regular basis;
- confidentiality; and
- openness to new ideas, flexibility and accessibility to staff.

One of the most important aspects of supervision is the leader's ability to work with staff in ways which optimise adult learning styles. Early childhood leaders need to understand that adults possess unique characteristics which differentiate them from children as learners. Examples of these characteristics are readiness, attitude, motivation, previous experiences and autonomy. Adult learning is grounded in experience, that is, it is focused on problem solving and on the relevance of process (Kolb, 1984). Supervisory styles which emphasise the links between theory, research and practice and encourage immediate application of new learning will help reduce the frustration that adult learners experience and help them to gain new knowledge and skills. Such a style will encourage staff to move beyond basic understanding of concepts and practices to more sophisticated approaches to information processing such as analysis, synthesis and evaluation of ideas and practices, in other words, to become a reflective practitioner.

The following principles have been suggested as central when considering teaching and learning techniques and processes when working with adults in a situation of learning (Albert & Einstein, 1986). Adults learn more effectively when:

- they are involved in the learning process, responsible for getting their own needs met, having the opportunity to build on existing skills in self-direction and decision making;
- their previous knowledge, skills and experience are utilised, with the leader encouraging other staff to help members within the team;
- their immediate concerns and problems are focused upon in

ways which result in new information, skills, insights and solutions that can be applied to their current situation;

- appropriate and varied teaching methods are used such as group discussions, brainstorming, role playing, problem solving and providing feedback as effective training strategies;
- a democratic atmosphere is established and maintained through the leader's emphasis on equality, shared responsibility, cooperation and mutual respect; and
- staff are actively involved in the learning process and learn by doing as well as by reflective thinking.

Effective leaders can capitalise upon adult learning styles in their supervisory role by understanding the principles underpinning adult learning and by developing the necessary skills for working with adults in order to improve professional performance.

Effective supervisors will match the model of supervision to the needs and the stage of professional development of the team members. These stages have been described in Chapter 1. Katz (1977; 1995a) argues that the training and supervisory needs of early childhood staff change with experience. New and inexperienced staff will require more concrete support and technical assistance than more experienced staff. Staff who have gained a degree of experience are more likely to benefit from exchanging information and observations with other experienced staff from their own or other centres. Consultation with Children's Services Advisers and other specialist staff, such as psychologists and curriculum advisers can extend the knowledge and skills of staff who are maturing in the job. Those staff who have considerable experience are likely to benefit from networking with colleagues outside the centre and by participating in conferences and in-service training programs.

The effective supervisor will give some consideration to the form of supervision to which staff will be most receptive. For some staff, the one-to-one tutorial model might be the most effective way support their development. New and inexperienced staff are likely to benefit from supervisors who impart information, listen to concerns and anxieties and show support and understanding in a private consultation. An extension of the tutorial model is the supervisory group model where a small group of staff who are at a similar stage of professional development meet with the supervisor.

Both inexperienced and experienced staff may find the peer model of supervision more stimulating. Peer supervision involves the objective observation of a colleague's practice without making inferences, interpretations or assumptions about the interaction and then sharing and discussing those observations (Schiller, 1987). It is an appropriate form of supervision when staff relationships are based upon mutual trust and respect. Staff may choose to work in self-selected pairs or, alternatively, small groups of individuals may wish to participate in regularly scheduled peer conferences to discuss aspects of observed practice and interaction. The peer model provides an opportunity independent of the supervisor to discuss decisions, solve problems, share responsibility and support one another. Peer supervision can encourage staff to engage in reflective thinking about practice and therefore provide a continuing opportunity for professional development.

The team model of supervision enables members of specific teams, for example staff who work in a specific room, to evaluate the morale and task aspects of their performance in order to work more effectively. When the leader shares the supervisory responsibility with the team, she needs to ensure that the group possesses the necessary professional knowledge and skills, the essential communication skills to manage this delicate task and a willingness to request outside help if the problems identified are beyond the resources of the group.

This book focuses on the need for developing more qualified leaders in the early childhood field who will facilitate the professionalisation of the field by raising the quality of care and early education through the consistent provision of quality programs. One way of developing leadership potential is through improved supervision of students in practicum and existing staff. The position of 'second-in-charge' offers considerable scope for the leader to become a mentor to a suitable member of staff and for that person to gain valuable on-the-job training and experience which will nurture emerging leadership potential.

The second-in-charge: a special opportunity for leadership in an early childhood team

The position of second-in-charge or Assistant Coordinator has the potential to be a valuable training ground for becoming a coordinator of an early childhood centre. However, there are a number of features of the role which make it as challenging as that of the official leader. The second-in-charge is an administrative position which is characterised by role ambiguity and conflict and where the level of responsibility fluctuates between shared and sole responsibility. It is a situation where the staff member is sometimes the official leader (on a short-term or longer term basis when the designated leader is absent) and sometimes a member of the team. The position of second-in-charge is usually filled by a staff member chosen by the leader. This is a good example of a situation where the principles of delegation should be applied by the leader to ensure that the most suitable staff member is selected for the task. The demands of the position call for sensitivity, flexibility and understanding on the part of the incumbent, the leader and the rest of the team.

There are three features of the role of the second-in-charge:

- to support the leader by obtaining cooperation and collaboration of team members in the operation and administration of the centre;
- to support the team in achieving its goals while maintaining positive working relationships; and
- to meet one's own needs for affection, belonging, self-esteem and competence.

At times, these may appear mutually exclusive and contradictory as well as impossible to achieve. However, the essence of the position is the provision of commitment to the delivery of efficient and effective early childhood programs. It is not about fulfilling power needs by controlling the team or sabotaging the leader's efforts or getting involved in centre politics. It is an opportunity to play a positive role at an administrative level for those staff members who are interested in achieving their full potential. The second-in-charge position is an opportunity to gain a broader perspective on the operation of an early childhood centre and the early childhood industry, to develop a broader background of skills and experience in terms of career openings. Any staff member who is interested in shared decision making and responsibility, team building, managing conflict, building trust and supporting the administrative structure of a centre is a potential candidate for a second-in-charge position because these are the skills that are demanded in the position.

When considering the position of second-in-charge, it is important to look at it from the perspective of professional career development. Both the training organisations and the unions who determine the award structures are aware of the current discrepancies in the qualifications, experience, roles, responsibilities and financial remuneration of personnel employed in the early childhood field. Efforts are being made to standardise designated positions with required specialisations, roles and responsibilities and essential competencies being spelt out clearly and associated with particular awards. The position of second-in-charge is in the process of becoming a designated position and it is probable that, in the future, aspiring leaders will be expected to have had some experience at a centre in this position. Although not mandatory at the moment, some experience as a second-in-charge is regarded favourably by potential employers who are interested in the capabilities of applicants for positions of leadership.

The changes in the award structures are likely to result in alterations to the leader's roles and responsibilities. An emphasis on administration in terms of the leader's contribution to long term planning, staff training and development and policy formulation will leave little time for any leader to have a large input into the day-to-day running of the early childhood centre. It is not inconceivable that the second-in-charge will take on increasing responsibility for the daily operation and administration of the centre. This scenario may witness designated administrative leaders becoming more isolated from the daily concerns of the centre. It may be the second-in-charge's responsibility to maintain the link between the leader, the team, the children and parents, and to keep the leader apprised of the current status of the centre by providing information and advice on the tasks, resources, opportunities and problems within the centre.

As with other aspects of working in early childhood, there has been little opportunity for orientation or training for those people who undertake second-in-charge positions. Most people have to 'learn on the job' to discover what the job is actually about, what roles and responsibilities are entailed and what skills are needed. In some cases, the second-in-charge has to fulfil her allocated duties as well as take on the extra duties associated with this administrative position. It is not surprising that many people in these positions experience high levels of stress and loss of morale when they think that their performance is not up to standard or if their relationships with their colleagues appear to deteriorate. The second-in-charge and the designated leader need to understand the key factors for successful leadership, the relationship between leadership and team performance and the communication skills which are essential to undertake the role effectively.

What are some of the difficulties associated with the position of second-in-charge? Apart from the lack of opportunity for training, the absence of a standardised job description or specification creates problems for leaders and their assistants. Some leaders willingly share authority, power, information and provide a time allocation for the extra administrative duties assumed by the second-in-charge. In this situation, they are afforded a genuine experience of the leadership position during the leader's absence. Other leaders are not interested in any real delegation to the second-in-charge, refusing to share real responsibilities and information, expecting any extra duties to be absorbed as part of the normal workload. The second-in-charge is only a token leader in the designated leader's absence. There is little uniformity in the provision of financial remuneration for those staff who accept the extra responsibilities associated with this position. The absence of formal channels of communication between the leader and second-in-charge can lead to difficulties in the mutual understanding of roles and responsibilities and expectations about financial remuneration for the higher duties.

A group of early childhood personnel who have been nominated as second-in-charge at their centres identified the following difficulties which appear to be inherent in the position at present. They are:

- lack of appropriate training and orientation for the position so that a complete understanding of the range of administrative duties associated with the position is developed;
- lack of a standardised job description which is associated with appropriate and mandated levels of financial remuneration;
- lack of allocation of an additional minimum time of three hours per week for administration in addition to two hours of planning time;
- lack of an operational definition of the parameters of delegated authority;
- lack of the mandatory employment of a reliever in the leader's absence;
- lack of ongoing involvement with the leader on certain policy and decision-making issues; and
- lack of on-going opportunity to participate in the wider early childhood profession.

Without such support, the potential for conflict between the leader and the second-in-charge was perceived by this group as high. Among the potential sources of conflict identified were:

- lack of leader support for decisions made in the leader's absence;
- few clearly defined roles and responsibilities;
- different ways of doing things;
- insufficient information provided;
- unwritten expectations;
- different values, ethics and interpretations of situations; and
- the leader feeling threatened by the second-in-charge's initiatives.

Lack of role definition and authority were considered to create the potential for conflict with the rest of the team when the second-in-charge was elevated to the position of responsibility in the designated leader's absence. Two major difficulties were identified here. Firstly, the team may not accept and challenge the second-in-charge's decisions and authority in the leader's absence. This sometimes relates to a difference of opinion about the necessity for qualified as opposed to experienced but unqualified staff being nominated as second-in-charge. One of the major problems faced by designated leaders, including the second-in-charge, is that they may not be recognised by the staff on unofficial levels as the leader. Someone else may have been subtly chosen as the unofficial leader by the staff. Such a person may be given unofficial power, the right to make decisions on behalf of the staff group and draw unquestioning support from the staff on an informal basis. A designated leader may need to earn the respect of staff by demonstrating relevant expertise, skills or knowledge and by gaining the support of staff through staff recognising the desirability and benefits of personal characteristics, resources and relationships in the early childhood context. Simply having an official position of leadership does not necessarily mean that the staff group will acknowledge and support the person in that position. In some cases, authority over, respect by and support from staff is earned through the way in which one fulfils the role.

Secondly, there is the issue of maintaining confidentiality. There have been instances when a member of the team has confided in the second-in-charge who then considered that it was her moral obligation to inform the leader. This is an example of an ethical dilemma for which a professional code of ethics should provide guidelines. An apparent breach of trust can have destructive outcomes on the future relationship with the team, with the second-in-charge being rejected as a member of the team when she no longer holds the leadership position. The impact on the second-in-charge's relationship with the team as a result of the varying levels of authority associated with the position was of concern to the group.

Although there are a number of other difficulties associated with this position there are many positive aspects to the role. Participation in a team in this capacity was perceived as building one's self-esteem and enhancing one's job satisfaction through the opportunity to provide input at a different level. The chance to demonstrate and develop one's leadership potential, gain experience and knowledge and to change people's perception about personal capacities were viewed as positive outcomes of accepting the extra responsibility. Awareness about the possible pitfalls and pressures of leadership responsibility is important because it allows individuals to develop the knowledge and skills necessary to undertake the position in the future. In terms of the overall team, a competent second-in-charge is essential to act as a backup in any emergency or unplanned absence by the leader. It is a logical and rational way of sharing the responsibility for helping the team to work effectively.

In summary, team building and effective team leadership usually result in high quality interaction between team members and the leader which increases trust and openness, the development of interpersonal relationships, joint goal setting, clarification of roles and responsibilities and analysis of the appropriate processes related to the team's purpose. The team approach to work in early childhood centres can also assist in staff development and in meeting the challenge of change because it provides the backdrop of support for and commitment to quality service delivery.

6

Initiating and implementing change

Change is one of the few certainties in life! It is a natural phenomenon in all aspects of our lives. Given that human beings experience so much change in their day-to-day lives, it can be difficult to understand why the process of change presents such a threat to some people. Indeed, one of the certainties about change is that it will be resisted by many people. Change occurs in individuals, organisations and in societies. Change at any of these levels will necessitate change in the others. Decisions usually involve change because the process of implementation requires change in individual attitudes and skills as well as organisational policies and procedures. Therefore, change is an inevitable, on-going process.

Change is also necessary. Growth is a result of change and illustrates the capacity of an individual or organisation to respond to the environment, to adapt, to be flexible, to question traditional or established practices, methods or ideas in order to develop new knowledge and ways of applying that knowledge. It is a means of sustaining individual and organisational survival.

The early childhood field has undergone a period of acute and chronic change where there have been many pressures for rapid and extensive changes over an extended period of time. Much uncertainty and unpredictability still exists for practitioners as the early childhood profession attempts to accommodate rapid social change and develop services and programs that are adaptive, flexible and responsive to community needs. While some members of the field perceive the current situation to be challenging and stimulating and ripe with future benefits, others view current events as a threat to themselves and the field, to be avoided and resisted at all costs. In both responses to change, emotions are aroused. Positive emotions tend to be associated with positive responses with change perceived as beneficial and a challenge. Negative emotions tend to be associated with negative responses with change perceived as stressful and destructive. The leader has to ensure that their early childhood service is viable under current and anticipated future conditions as well as meeting the needs for support and strengthened team morale.

The role of the leader has become instrumental in managing change in organisations with leaders in recent times being referred to as 'agents of change' (Daughtrey & Ricks, 1994). As with leaders of other organisations, early childhood leaders are expected to ensure efficient use of resources to meet present demands while at the same time finding ways to guarantee the long-term survival and effectiveness of the early childhood service. In terms of change, effectiveness means the ability to adapt to changing circumstances (Carnall, 1995). The planning for and implementation of change is one of the major challenges for today's leaders in early childhood (Saracho, 1992). Leadership for change requires vision and inspiration, careful planning, decision-making skills, effective communication, confident conflict management and sensitive handling of people involved in or affected by the change. The extent to which change is well planned, sensitively handled, appropriately timed and sufficiently resourced or a loosely conceived, loosely implemented program of action will depend on the leader's understanding of the process of change and its implementation in an organisational setting.

For those early childhood practitioners who have not thought about the essence of change the following general points are useful for understanding where and how it fits into personal and professional life. Change:

- is inevitable;
- is necessary;
- is a process;
- occurs in individuals, organisations and societies;
- can be anticipated and planned for;
- is a highly emotional process;
- can cause tension and stress;
- is resisted by many people;

- can be adjusted to by individuals and groups with the support of the leader;
- entails developmental growth in attitudes and skills, policies and procedures; and
- is best facilitated on the basis of diagnosed needs.

When considering change, the leader must recognise that the organisation does not exist solely for the purpose of testing out new ideas. Prior experience with ad hoc approaches to change, where change has been introduced for change's sake, has left many of those involved feeling ambiguous about or resistant to future change. This is because organisational effectiveness and viability are rarely enhanced through ad hoc changes. Successful organisations have become so because their leaders have ensured that they have adjusted continually to the demands, both in terms of opportunities and constraints, that their social, political and economic environments have made upon them. These leaders understand that the organisation exists to benefit its mission and to achieve its objectives. Therefore, change should only be considered if it is thought to be effective in furthering the organisation's mission and objectives.

Organisational strength is a function of the mix of and balance between two major forces: bureaucratisation and innovation. Bureaucratisation refers to the need to establish ritual, routine and predictable ways of doing things and is a means of ensuring organisational stability. Rules and regulations, standard procedures, division of labour and the internal structural hierarchy are examples of bureaucratic forces. Overemphasis on the traditional and established ways of doing things can result in failure to perceive the need for change, lack of action or inadequate action which comes too late. Sometimes organisations continue to uphold policies and practices, not because they are the most effective or efficient ways to do things now, or even that they were the best ways to do things in the past, but simply because they were done in the past.

Innovation refers to organisational responses to any environmental demand and is the force which gives the organisation its adaptability, flexibility and responsiveness. Changes in structure (for example, new staff groupings), communication channels and processes (such as who reports what to whom, when and how) and changes in behaviour (such as in leadership style) illustrate innovation in an organisation. Overemphasis on innovation can lead to a haphazard approach to change, premature change and blind imitation of certain policies and practices of similar organisations (an attitude of 'if they're doing it, it must be right, so we'll do it too'). The leader must ensure that decisions which are sufficiently innovative are based upon diagnosed needs as well as adequate bureaucratisation in order to meet the demands of task performance and team morale.

Types of change in organisations

Change in organisations occurs in a variety of ways and involves different levels of significance for those affected by the change. Organisations, such as early childhood centres, are dynamic in that the people, hierarchies, structures and systems are continually evolving. The pursuit of new knowledge and experiences, more efficient methods and more effective functions by the members of any organisation produces incremental change where small changes are introduced into and absorbed by the system on a day-to-day basis. These small changes often go unnoticed until a substantial difference is discerned by a staff member. Simple changes to the early childhood curriculum or routines are examples of incremental changes to which little attention is given. A series of incremental changes, whether planned or unintentional, can result in a major organisational shift in an unwanted direction if it is not adequately monitored.

Induced change is another means by which change is effected in an organisation. Induced change involves a conscious decision to implement a change in people, processes, programs, structures and systems. Participation in a conference or in-service training program can stimulate the desire to change an aspect of an early childhood service, such as the parent program, the curriculum or the staff's child management practices. Induced change can involve different levels of significance. It can be routine, to meet a crisis, innovative and, more rarely, transformational (as explained below).

Routine change is very common and is effected by the leader and team members on a daily basis in response to problem situations. The aim is to restore the status quo. Routine changes are designed to improve the quality of the program, to meet the needs of children and parents, to enhance cooperation between staff and to reduce conflict.

Crisis change, as the name suggests, is any response to an unexpected occurrence in the centre. Due to time constraints, the leader is likely to make a quick decision without consulting the team members. Team members usually do not object to the demands of change in a crisis and are willing to accept an authoritarian decision by the leader in order to meet the needs of the situation. An exception to this is where the leader has procrastinated about or deferred necessary decision making. Staff members may not be supportive of an executive decision under these circumstances. Crisis change can occur as a result of unexpected staff resignation, illness or absence, unexpected changes in physical or financial conditions or unexpected needs of children. Failure to recognise the need for change can precede and precipitate a crisis change.

Innovative change can be a result of creative problem solving or trial and error where the leader and team members are seeking easier, faster and more effective ways to further the centre's mission and meet its objectives. Innovative change is more likely to occur under the team leadership of a highly supportive, committed and goal-oriented staff group. New centre operation hours to meet the needs of local parents and children is an example of innovative change. Decision making for innovative change involves two processes, those of initiation and implementation (Zaltman, Duncan & Holbek, 1973). Initiation includes knowledge awareness, the formation of positive attitudes towards the change and the actual decision to change. Implementation includes the initial introduction and planned execution of the change plus continued, sustained implementation of the change. However, Hasenfeld (1992) cautions that the decision-making process for the initiation and implementation of change rarely follows a rational and logical sequence from problem recognition to evaluation of alternatives to the adoption of a solution. Early childhood professionals need to combine understanding about decision-making processes with awareness about factors that can make innovative change appear a chaotic event.

Transformational change, where the form of an organisation is radically altered, occurs at crisis point when the survival of the organisation calls for drastic action. This type of change is most likely to occur if the organisation fails to respond to the demands of the environment due to an overemphasis on either bureaucratisation or innovation. The necessity for routine, minor crisis and innovative changes may have been ignored by the leader and the team. It is interesting to note that transformational change is occurring in the early childhood field with the assimilation of pre-school programs into child-care services. The pressures on staff involved in transformational change are enormous and the potential for stress and burnout is high.

Change and the individual

Effective leaders understand that any organisational change can have a major impact on the lives of those involved or affected by it. It is not uncommon for people to react to change with anxiety, uncertainty and stress, even those who are fully committed to change (Carnall, 1990). The magnitude of the change will determine the amount of stress that is generated. Stress and its management are very important for change to be implemented successfully (Harvey, 1990). Conflict is often the impetus for change and should not be avoided in professional situations. However, both conflict and stress need to be managed intelligently by the leader (Selye, 1975) because there are definite links between these and self-esteem and performance. While some stress can challenge and motivate individuals, too much stress lowers performance and self-esteem. Leaders need to develop the art of managing stress levels in such a way that optimal performance and associated high levels of self-esteem are produced in the individual.

Change at work can challenge the individual's sense of professional self which has been constructed over time through their interaction with the task and colleagues. The competent accomplishment of tasks becomes routine with experience and, for many staff, change threatens their sense of competence and mastery of the situation. This may lead to staff questioning the meaning of their work. These factors can evoke defensive reactions to suggestions of change as well as active and passive opposition and resistance to the implementation of any change. It is the leader's responsibility to overcome this tendency by presenting any impending change in ways that permit staff members to see it as a new opportunity that is consistent with existing views about self and which do not threaten routines or question their established perceptions about work. Leaders also need to be aware that any personal concerns or lack of confidence about their ability to facilitate change in the organisation are likely to result in the adoption of a more autocratic style of leadership which will decrease the team's ability to respond positively to the change.

As has been discussed in Chapter 2, those individuals with positive self-concepts and high levels of self-esteem are more likely to have a positive attitude to change and to respond to the demands of change in a creative way. This type of individual has been described by Dunphy (1986) as 'The Learning Person' with the other end of the continuum being described as 'The Self-Defeating Person'. This is an important concept in understanding change because change is inevitable. The Learning Person perceives change as an opportunity for growth and development, approaches the situation with confidence and enthusiasm and is willing to learn new skills to become competent in the new situation. Knowing that change is inevitable, energy and time is put into preparing for change. Personal effectiveness and creativity are enhanced and a more positive attitude to future personal and organisational change is developed. Organisations which are made up of 'Learning Persons' become 'Learning Organisations' where individual members are receptive to each other's ideas and are committed to learning and growing together.

On the other hand, the 'Self-Defeating' Person, who believes that change will threaten her security or demand skills which she cannot attain, erroneously believes that change can be avoided, forestalled or even stopped. Energy and time is put into opposing and resisting change. Stress levels escalate, conflict within the organisation increases. A corresponding deterioration in performance, relationships with other staff and self-esteem is inevitable. Withdrawal and alienation from the team and organisational goals is an eventual outcome of this process. In this situation, the leader needs to work with the individual to develop self-esteem and confidence to meet the demands of the new situation. As well, the leader needs to assist the individual to understand the role of change in organisational survival as well as individual survival.

A commitment to personal and professional development on the part of staff members is essential to meet the requirements for change in the early childhood profession. Effective leaders accept that staff members have the right to be cautious about anything new but not the right to not grow and develop. Furthermore, nobody in the early childhood field has the right to stop others from growing and developing. Staff development programs help foster self-esteem and create individuals who are more resistant to threat. The leader needs to help any 'Self-Defeating' members of staff develop into 'Learning Persons' so that resistance to change is minimised and they are able to approach change with interest and enthusiasm.

Sources of resistance to change

Every early childhood centre is different and therefore will experience resistance to change from different sources. However, there are some common sources of resistance to change which can be identified. It is the leader's responsibility to identify what sources of resistance are operating in the centre and to find antidotes or ways of overcoming such resistance. The following sources of resistance to change have been identified in early childhood settings.

- Fear about personal future in a changed environment is a major source of resistance. Individual staff members fear the unknown and may be anxious about losing their jobs, having their salary reduced, losing status, the inability to perform a new job, taking on new responsibilities, undergoing new training, changes in social relationships or possible relocation (Daughtrey & Ricks, 1994);
- Ideological factors such as changes in values and belief systems which may affect program goals, such as moving from an adult-centred, curriculum-driven program to a child-centred developmental program;
- Individual personalities such as 'Self-Defeating' staff members with low self-esteem and people who prefer routine and predictability;
- Misunderstandings about the need for, the purpose of, and the scope and the ramifications of the change;
- Lack of trust in the leader where the staff do not believe that the leader has their best interests at heart;
- Different assessments or points of view about the proposed change and its effects on the established team culture;
- Self-interest where an individual perceives the change involving loss of benefits or little personal pay-off;
- Lack of knowledge to understand the proposed change;
- Technological factors where technology requires new skills or new ways of doing the job;
- Lack of ownership where change is imposed from without; and
- Excessive change in the immediate past or demands for sudden change.

Dealing with resistance to change

The way in which the leader approaches staff resistance to change is an important issue in implementing any change. Fighting resistance, trying to overcome it with arguments, information, data and power is usually not successful because the resistance goes underground (Harvey, 1990). Using force to deal with resistance is likely to produce a desire for revenge where staff wait for an opportunity to get even. A better way to handle resistance is to encourage the full expression of concerns (Block, in McLennan, 1989). The goal is to get the staff to start expressing their fears, concerns and anxieties directly to the leader and each other and to stop any attempts at subterfuge and sabotage.

The following methods of dealing with resistance have been outlined by Daughtrey and Ricks (1994) and are useful for leaders of early childhood services because they draw on communication and problem-solving skills which have been highly developed in early childhood personnel in order to operate and administer an early childhood centre.

Communication and education

These methods can be used prior to and during the implementation of a change where lack of, or inaccurate, information increases stress levels and hinders staff members' perceptions of the benefits of the change. If individual staff members understand the rationale behind the change, they may be persuaded to accept the change. An important outcome of communication and education is that staff may assist with the implementation phase by providing accurate information to other staff members. Unless some other staff can be involved in communicating with and educating team members, it can become a very time-consuming activity for the leader, especially if large numbers of people are involved.

Participation and involvement

These methods can be used prior to and during the implementation phase where a leader wants to ensure team commitment to the proposed change, where the leader needs more information to design the change or where there are large numbers of possible resisters. The team is invited to provide advice to the leader and to help design and implement the change. Participation helps reduce stress and fears and it acts as a motivator by increasing self-esteem. Resisters are more likely to contribute if they believe that they can have some control over the process. Participating and involved staff can contribute to integrating all the available, relevant information into the proposal which will assist in refining and enhancing commitment to the final outcome. The only disadvantage is that poorly supervised participants may design an inappropriate change which can be costly and time-consuming to rectify should it be implemented. The leader needs to monitor the team's direction and contribution to ensure that the change is consistent with the centre's mission and objectives.

Facilitation and support

These methods can be used where staff are resisting change. While this is time-consuming, costly and may be unsuccessful, it is the only option a leader has to deal with adjustment problems. Attention is focused on staff members' concerns about task performance and relationships. The leader employs listening skills, conflict-resolution skills, problem-solving skills and stress management skills to strengthen the level of trust in the group. Acknowledgement of and empathy for the difficulties of undergoing change is essential. Support through training and access to other resources needs to be made available.

Negotiation and agreement

These methods can be used where it is obvious that someone is going to forfeit certain current benefits or experience extra burdens, or when the team has a lot of power to resist the change. The leader needs to offer incentives to actual or potential resisters or work out some form of trade-off where special benefits are guaranteed if the change is not blocked. A difficulty can be that the early childhood leader may have little to offer in terms of special incentives and benefits because she may not have the power to provide financial and time in lieu rewards. Prestige in terms of nomination for the position of second-in-charge may be a reward for some staff members.

Effective implementation of change

Staff tend to go through stages to cope with change. Firstly, they may deny that a need for change exists and may try to defend the status quo. Much energy can be devoted to resistance if staff members have not been prepared adequately for the change or given enough time to adjust to the realities of the situation. As staff come to perceive that change is inevitable and necessary, with sufficient support from the leader they begin to let go of the past and focus on the future. Staff will then start to adapt to the new requirements but may find this period frustrating as they may not have the level of skill and competence to meet the new demands. Ongoing mutual support from the team and the leader is essential to move the staff through this stage and to ensure the long-term success of the change. Finally, as the change is incorporated into the personal repertoire of the staff and into the organisational system, it is accepted as a normal and routine part of the program.

The leader can set the conditions for the successful implementation of a change by following a three-step model which was proposed by Lewin (1974) and described by Schein (in McLennan, 1989). Change should be understood by leaders as a people-oriented process which involves 'unfreezing', changing and 'refreezing' attitudes and behaviours.

Unfreezing

This is the process of motivating staff to change by making them aware of the need for it and making them receptive to the change. The staff must be persuaded that the present situation is ineffective and that they have a professional responsibility to respond to the situation to restore the expected level of effectiveness. A sense of psychological safety can be tapped by the leader conveying to staff her confidence in their ability to cope with the change. The leader must address any barriers to and sources of resistance to change at this point. A common mistake many leaders make is to introduce change when the team is not sufficiently 'unfrozen', that is, receptive to change.

Changing

This refers to the developing of new attitudes and behaviours on the basis of diagnosed need, new information or cognitive redefinition where new ways of looking at old information are adopted. The essence of changing is to ensure that the staff engage in the new behaviour or situation and start to experiment with the change. This is a transitional stage where learning, risk taking and creativity are required. The more the staff interact with the change, the faster it will be integrated into accepted, normal patterns at work. The leader needs to provide feedback about how well the staff are doing in effecting improvements in achieving the mission and objectives, improving the strategies, tasks, structures and team culture.

Refreezing

This occurs when the staff have accepted the change to such a point where they support it as a normal part of daily life. The leader needs to stabilise the change by restoring a sense of equilibrium to the work environment but at a higher level of effectiveness. The process of 'refreezing' helps eliminate the feelings of chaos and lack of control that some staff experience during change. The leader needs to provide support for the change, reward the staff for their efforts to meet the demands of change and review and evaluate the effects so that any adjustments can be made. Efforts need to be made to ensure that staff members are supported in the rebuilding of their self-esteem. If the conditions are not stabilised following the introduction of a change, the staff might revert to the old way and the change will be short-lived or abandoned. The leader's inability to 'refreeze' the changed circumstances accounts for many attempts at change which fail.

Helping staff cope with change

Fear and uncertainty about change can lower staff morale and lower their performance level. However, staff members can be supported through periods of change by a sensitive leader who can ease adjustment to new demands and enhance self-esteem in the process. These guidelines for early childhood leaders which have been adapted from suggestions by Schrag, Nelson and Siminowsky (1985) are called the 'Six Cs of Change'.

Challenge

Help staff perceive change as a challenge not a threat by developing staff morale, open communication and encouraging a mutually supportive team approach to work.

Communicate

Keep staff informed. Fear of the unknown, lack of information or misinformation leads to resistance and lack of trust in the leader.

Empathise with staff members' real experiences and problems with change. Don't ignore or trivialise them.

Commitment

Involve staff in the diagnosis of the need for change, the planning, design and implementation of the change. Participation and involvement in decision making and problem solving ensures a high level of commitment. In this way, staff 'own' the change and it has not been imposed from without.

Control

Help staff feel that they are not powerless in the face of change and that, through participation and involvement, they will be able to influence the course of the change. Allow for some flexibility to incorporate staff ideas and feedback. Train staff in the skills of negotiation.

Confidence

Build confident, resilient staff who do not read any implications about their worth into change. Help staff realistically identify and feel comfortable with their strengths and weaknesses. Focus on self-awareness and self-acceptance while at the same time encouraging staff to engage in personal and professional development.

Connect

Network with other individuals and organisations who are undergoing change to help staff develop awareness of the inevitability of change and a more sophisticated approach to adapting to change. Extend the team's support network by linking up with colleagues and peers in the field. Ask for outside assistance if necessary.

Developing leadership for change

Leadership for change is a key role for early childhood professionals who are committed to the provision of high quality services for the community. While many of the factors which relate to effective leadership have been outlined in previous chapters, the demands of facilitating change in the early childhood field require several additional abilities. Hersey and Blanchard (1988) suggest

138

that there are three general skills that leaders need in order to facilitate change in an organisation:

- Diagnosing (a cognitive skill with which the leader assesses the gap between the present situation and future needs);
- Adapting (a behavioural skill in which the leader modifies behaviour and other resources to solve the problem of meeting future needs); and
- Communicating (a process skill used by the leader to communicate clear objectives and direction to others).

In addition, Schoonover and Dalziel (1986) argue that the effective leader should take into account the organisation's previous history of change when considering the timing of the change. Positive or negative experiences with change in the past, as well as the length of time that an organisation has been experiencing change and the significance or magnitude of change that has been required, affect the organisation's readiness to accept further change. The organisation's previous experience of change can act as a barrier to the implementation of necessary changes. Given that the early childhood field has been undergoing a long period of change with little preparation of its workers and few skilled agents of change, there is likely to be a high level of resistance to the introduction of further change. The effective leader will analyse the critical barriers to change and plan any innovation in small, unintimidating steps which will minimise stress levels of those who are involved with or affected by the change.

To implement a change, the leader will first ensure that the team clearly understands the need for and the benefits of the change, will communicate the objectives so that the team has a clear sense of purpose, will provide broad guidelines for achieving the objectives (such as a step-by-step plan), will encourage team participation to clarify the needed change and provide detailed information relevant to the change and, finally, will provide feedback and some form of reward for those who participated in the implementation of the change.

The essence of the leader's role in facilitating change is to set, clarify and focus on the values underpinning the needed change, to support the team's task accomplishment through calculated risk taking and problem solving, to design processes and procedures which will support manageable action and to support people in the development of confidence and skills. This is not any easy task but it is an essential one. Change is about learning by the leader and by the team. It is possible that some changes will not be effected or will be short-lived. An effective leader will not be overly concerned with failure or avoid becoming involved with possible future change but will reassess the situation and try again. Commitment to change in order to further the professionalisation of the early childhood field is another hallmark of the effective leader.

Features of successful change programs

To complete this study of leadership and change, the leader needs to be able to identify the following characteristics in her plans to implement change and increase the probability of its success.

- Clear objectives which provide a sense of purpose for the team;
- A realistic and limited scope—start small and build up as small changes are successful and the team becomes more receptive to change;
- Informed awareness by team members about the role of change in personal, professional and organisational development and survival;
- Selection of appropriate intervention strategies which are consistent with the organisation's culture;
- Good timing and appropriate pace—ensure change is not introduced too early or too late, too slow or too fast;
- A sense of ownership through participation of all involved especially resisters;
- Support from key power groups especially top management;
- Involvement of existing power structures such as the second-in-charge and lobby groups;
- Open assessment or diagnosis before any attempts to initiate change begin;
- Support of the majority of staff to minimise resistance;
- Support of competent staff to optimise the probability of success;
- Training and other necessary support available;
- A framework where new policies, procedures and practices can be integrated with existing and established ones;
- A protocol for continued evaluation; and
- Adequate rewards to reinforce the change such as feedback and public recognition.

In conclusion, early childhood services have been criticised recently for their apparent inability to respond to the demands of change. While the field has been responsive to change on the basis of crisis, it appears that it has yet to develop the capacity to engage in innovative change, that is, where early childhood leaders exhibit the motivation to overcome obstacles, to counteract sources of resistance to change and to mobilize both internal and external resources which can support change. The traditional conservatism of the early childhood field ultimately will mitigate its long-range survival and viability. However, if attitudes to change become more positive, the future can hold exciting possibilities for children, parents and the staff who are associated with early childhood services.

7

Leadership and the research connection

Until recently, the early childhood field has not been concerned with developing a research ethos (Finkelstein, 1988), with interest in research generally being confined to child development and its application to care and educational settings. Early childhood practitioners have not considered research to be a part of their professional role and historically have been content to rely on academic staff from a variety of disciplines within universities to pursue new knowledge and apply it to child-care and early education. A historical division between research and academic staff and early childhood professionals has led to the latter becoming recipients of others' advice and consumers rather than producers of research. With their reluctance to regard themselves as intellectuals with a responsibility and capacity for scientific enquiry, early childhood professionals themselves have perpetuated the perception that they are a lower status group mainly concerned with practice rather than theory (Almy, 1988).

The role of research in the professionalisation of the early childhood field generally has focused on improving the environment of development for young children, with little interest shown in identifying and examining factors related to the development and activities of those adults who work with them (Jorde-Bloom & Sheerer, 1992). However, leadership is currently considered to incorporate the ability to understand and apply research findings to early childhood programs, and the ability to design and implement a research project within a centre or service (Jorde-Bloom & Sheerer, 1992). Eminent psychologist and advocate for early childhood Jacqueline Goodnow (1989) argues that research is one of the most effective ways to optimise the care and education of young children as well as professionalising the image of the field. She recommends the setting of research priorities into a range of aspects related to the early childhood field including marketing, national standards and national policy issues. Goodnow (1989) and Almy (1988) challenge early childhood professionals to identify and strengthen the growing professionalisation of the field with the scientific application of research findings to care and educational settings for young children, thereby linking practice to professional knowledge.

In opting out of the research role, early childhood practitioners have lost a valuable tool for change which has distanced them from the issue of how to influence others to think and act (Almy, 1988). This means that their ability to initiate and implement change on their own behalf and from their specialised knowledge base is limited. This lack of involvement in research also raises questions about whether the early childhood field meets one of the fundamental criteria for professionalism (Silin, 1988) if the basis of early childhood practitioners' work is merely putting into practice a knowledge base which has been generated by researchers from other professions. Researchers from many other disciplines such as psychology have a goal of increasing knowledge and are mainly interested in what is, not what ought to or could be. The early childhood field has a responsibility to meet the challenge of effecting change and needs to go beyond the descriptive to the predictive and appropriately responsive. However, many early childhood professionals also tend to resist change which is suggested by research findings because much of the tradition and many of the practices of the early childhood field are based on professionally socialised attitudes, beliefs and values which are ingrained and hard to change under any circumstances, let alone on the recommendation of research conducted by an 'outsider' who would not be able to empathise with the idiosyncratic constraints of the early childhood field.

Because there is little sense of ownership of research relevant for the early childhood field, a gap exists between those who conduct research and those practitioners who could and should use the findings in their work with children and families. Practitioners have a vital role to play in initiating and implementing change in any society where informed action is based on critical enquiry and reflective judgement. Early childhood practitioners need to move beyond enlisting and relying on research programs of academic educators and psychologists (Biber, 1988) and assume responsibility for conducting the research which will provide direction for the field in the future. This will require a shift away from traditional conceptual simplicity which is concrete, particular and not necessarily valid to a scientific interdisciplinary approach to knowledge and thinking which is theoretical, general and rational.

Unfortunately, the early childhood field, as in other systems of education, suffers from a lack of understanding and subsequently a lack of interest in the relationship between research and innovation and change. An uneasy relationship exists between individuals engaged in practice in the early childhood field and those engaged in research (Katz, 1977; Takanishi, 1986). Early childhood professionals can find themselves caught between the push for change and the pull of tradition, reactive to the variety of trends and counter-trends that access to information has enabled. However, the field has been undergoing rapid change throughout the world and is under pressure to address many pressing problems faced by children, families and professionals. The greatest challenge facing the early childhood field today is to find new ways to encounter and understand early childhood development, care and education and to be innovative in the application of new knowledge to assist early childhood practitioners, administrators and leaders to improve the quality of service and enhance the quality of life for children, families and professionals.

What is research and what can it offer those who care for and educate young children?

Research is a basic tool for advancing knowledge and stimulating change in attitudes, values and practice, all of which are essential means for progressing the early childhood field. Research can help explain the current status of the field by looking at and reflecting upon the past. It also contributes to the impetus to develop new ideas and directions. Research is a means of evaluating the impact of a variety of ecological contexts upon children's development and learning as well as professional practice. Research can be used to influence the design of broad social policies. In short, research can provide early childhood professionals with a comprehensive, systematic, rational basis for understanding child development in a broad sense, and for practical action. It is also a means to staff development through increased professional learning.

The demands on early childhood professionals are high, in that they are required to provide quality services which meet the range of developmental needs of children in ways which are socially and culturally relevant. Early childhood is generally recognised as a prime time for development and learning, with society holding certain assumptions and expectations regarding the types of experiences young children need to be exposed to and shielded from. Early childhood professionals are expected to extend their contribution to the development and welfare of children by meeting parents' needs for information, support and education. The early childhood professional is the agent who is charged with the responsibility for making decisions about the experiences which will optimise young children's development and learning (Schaffer, 1996), whether they are in a child-care centre, a pre-school or in a home-based context. All-in-all, they are expected to be responsive to the challenge of constant change in society. The key question is 'on what basis and with what information do early childhood practitioners make decisions about young children and their families?'

There are a range of sources of information and strategies (Mason & Bramble, 1989; Schaffer, 1996) which early childhood practitioners utilise in order to engage in responsible decision making and be responsive to the challenge of change. Powell and Stremmel (1989) argue that the leader of an early childhood centre has a large impact on the sources and variety of information that are available to staff, particularly those with little or no training. It is interesting to note that educators in general, and early childhood professionals in particular, have been reluctant and hesitant to use research as a basis of decision making but have tended to rely upon other sources of information as guidelines and reference points for decision making. Some of these sources have a number of disadvantages and are likely to result in poor quality and perhaps even inappropriate decisions for children, families and professionals alike.

One of the most common sources of information for decision making is personal opinion and intuition. This involves the use of a subjective viewpoint which is usually derived from personal values and experience as a guide to action and decision making.

As such, it needs to be treated with extreme caution. Under this broad umbrella of knowledge about development, care and education, early childhood professionals use a number of common expressions to rationalise their decisions. Among the more popular references are 'intuition' which may or may not have some basis in theory but which is often little more than a gut feeling that the exponent cannot justify on rational and logical grounds; 'common sense' which can be vague and often incorrect and fallible; 'in my experience' which may have been limited and/or unrepresentative of general experience; and 'in the best interests of the child/parent/staff member' which usually describes a personal opinion or dogma.

This subjective approach as an information source for decision making tends to be unhelpful because it is influenced by the prevailing moral and social climate, personal values, convictions and stereotypes, the psychological characteristics and personal histories of the decision maker and other political and ideological considerations. What is being used as a basis for decision making in this approach are personal mythologies about development, care and education. Inexperienced early childhood professionals are prone to relying on this source of information as a basis for action which is often well-intentioned but non-professional (Vander Ven, 1988).

Tradition or the justification of decisions and action by reference to historical or established practices is another major source of information used by early childhood practitioners, often to create barriers to and resist suggested changes. In this approach, expressions are used such as 'that's the way I was brought up and it didn't hurt me', 'we've always done it that way' and 'why change something that's working well. Leave well enough alone!'. Early childhood practitioners need to recognise that considerable differences exist from one period of time to another, as well as from one place to another. Attitudes and practices which were fashionable at one time or in a particular place lose popularity as more information becomes available and societies change. While traditional and established practices may have been defensible at one time, exponents of some of these approaches rarely appeal to rational, logical or scientific evidence as the basis of their claims. Rather, bold assertion of subjective assumptions and preconceptions about what is 'the best way' is the strength of the argument and there is usually little room for debate. Fear about the uncertainty of change may evoke the tendency to hang on to what is known or familiar. However, early childhood practitioners who use this as a basis for their decision making are likely to find themselves in a vulnerable situation professionally because their ideas and practices are out of touch with the rest of the community and the field.

Reference to 'The Expert' as a source of information for decision making is a common strategy used by early childhood professionals. There are many experts who have contributed to scientific knowledge about and understanding of development, care and education, such as Bowlby, Bronfenbrenner, Freud, Katz, Piaget, Spodek and Tizard to name a few. Then there are other experts who have professional credentials and background but who often rely on their personal charisma or reputation to capture the imagination of ordinary people. These experts, such as Dr Benjamin Spock and Dr T. Berry Brazelton, are able to exert influence on knowledge, understanding and practice in the popular culture. In the main, their contribution has been helpful and informative but it is essential that early childhood practitioners, who have had a tendency to defer to the 'experts in the field', do not simply take for granted the wisdom of these so-called experts from other disciplines, such as psychology, sociology, biology and history but closely examine the sources of their information and recommendations.

While early childhood practitioners have assumed that the interests of the field can be represented by contributions from more prestigious individuals and groups of professionals, the training of these experts leads to different perspectives on early childhood settings (Silin, 1988) and takes decision making and change out of the hands of early childhood practitioners. Moreover, the majority of experts have been men who are likely to have a very different perspective on the issues which are important to the overwhelming percentage of women who constitute the early childhood field. In addition, an expert's information and recommendations can be derived from a mixture of personal opinion and intuition, guesswork and informed hunches, folklore, work with small numbers of clinical cases and often the experience of rearing their own children. The proportion of reliable and valid scientific information from which claims are asserted may be small.

The other major source of information as a basis for decision making, which is available to but under-utilised by early childhood practitioners, is research. As described earlier, research is the systematic investigation of a problem or issue. For a service provider, research is a form of audit, examining and evaluating the system as a basis for good practice and benefiting consumers (Tripp, 1990). The information and knowledge derived from research has certain characteristics which give it advantages over other sources of information.

- Research is empirical. Conclusions are based on direct observations of relevant phenomena or from verifiable experience available to all.
- Research is systematic. Data are collected according to an explicit plan not on an ad hoc basis, dependent on personal biases or tendencies.
- Research is controlled. Studies are designed in such a way as to rule out all possible explanations except one.
- Research is basic and applied. The purpose of basic research is to develop a base of knowledge upon which theory can be built. Applied research is often designed to answer practical and useful questions, solve specific problems or provide information that is of immediate use.
- Research is qualitative and quantitative. Qualitative studies can provide descriptive data whereas quantitative data enable comparisons between groups or conditions. Qualitative data, used in conjunction with quantitative data, can help practitioners understand what the numbers mean.
- Research is public. The methodology and findings of studies are available for public scrutiny so that the work can be critically assessed and subsequently replicated by other researchers.

Research can provide early childhood practitioners with valid and reliable information on which they can confidently make new decisions, reaffirm previous decisions and initiate change. Such changes will not be on an ad hoc basis or 'change for change's sake' but will be changes based on a rational and logical basis. Unfortunately, Gibbs (1990) reports some disheartening research which indicates that the attitudes of those beginning early childhood studies change very little once they are in the early childhood profession. Early childhood practitioners need to be encouraged to value and incorporate research as a source of decision making in order to avoid becoming rigid, stereotyped and outdated in their attitudes. The outcome of such a research based approach should increase their professional development and effectiveness because personal bias will be reduced and mistakes minimised. Research, however, does not provide magical answers and there may be no one right answer to the questions asked or the problems posed. The answer more often than not may be 'it depends', that is, factors such as the individual, the type and composition of the group, the type of intervention and the local conditions will affect the interpretation of research outcomes. In addition, more questions and problems will be generated for future investigation than will be resolved by research but in this way the pool of knowledge relevant for early childhood practitioners will be expanded.

In Chapter 1, the relationship between stage of professional career development and leadership was explored. Vander Ven (1988) argues that early childhood practitioners who are at higher stages in professional career development, such as Stage 3—Informed, Stage 4—Complex and Stage 5—Influential, use more complex and sophisticated sources of information in their daily practice. They do not rely on common sense, their personal experience or simplistic applications of basic empirical knowledge and theory but rather demonstrate progressive thinking by utilising an interdisciplinary knowledge base (that is underpinned by scientific research) and which is interpreted in the light of clinical experience.

Spodek (Spodek et al., 1988) has put forward an interesting point of view in his assertion that, although early childhood professionals do not perceive themselves as researchers, they can be defined as researchers because they are continually processing information gathered as they work with children and families. Using the data collected prior to, during and following decision making, Spodek suggests that they construct their own implicit theories on which to base future action. These theories are extracted out of their own clinical experience and practice and are not developed and tested by researchers for other disciplines. An effective leader in the early childhood field will base practice on information gained from scientific research as well as the intuitive theories that have been constructed from her own experience.

Why is research under-utilised by early childhood professionals?

The current situation in many early childhood centres, where practice may not reflect what research has discovered about development, care and education, is one which needs to be transformed quickly if the early childhood field is to gain professional credibility and status within the community. Given the slow progress of the adoption of a research orientation by the early childhood field, Clyde (1989) suggests that research needs to be encouraged by politicians and the public alike. However, she acknowledges that, regardless of the source of support for research, the early childhood field's limited awareness of and interest in research is a major obstacle to the meaningfulness and application of any research findings and recommendations.

It is evident that a gulf exists between research and practice in the early childhood field which results in research having little impact on early childhood services. Practitioners appear to be unaware of the need for and the benefits of new knowledge in relation to the improvement of professional practice. This situation would be unthinkable in other professions where it is an inherent expectation that professionals keep abreast of current research and developments in practice. Imagine how a medical practitioner or an engineer would be perceived if they were ignorant of, disregarded or discounted new research findings and failed to incorporate them into their work! It would be considered totally unacceptable by other members of the profession, consumers and the general public. However, relatively few members of the early childhood profession see it as their professional responsibility to keep up-to-date with the relevant research and other literature. Yet, the role of a leader is to communicate vision and implement ideas with the support of the team. Leaders of early childhood services have not yet understood that well-designed research is a reliable source of information where many of those new ideas can be found, developed, transformed or created.

It is not difficult to identify some of the reasons why research is under-utilised by early childhood professionals. Several of these are outlined below.

1 The professional socialisation which occurs in pre-service training has not generally included a focus on the role and value of research. Basic attitudes and values towards research have not been nurtured in the preparation of early childhood personnel. The emphasis has been on skill development for the practical aspects of working with children and operating services with little attempt to develop the skills required to understand and conduct research. The predominantly practice-oriented interests of early childhood practitioners appear to

have acted as an inhibitor to basic research in areas related to early childhood.

2   Early childhood professionals are often unaware of what type of research exists due to the practical orientation and limitations of current training. For some practitioners, the lack of training is the obstacle here. Many early childhood staff simply lack knowledge of what research is available because in general they do not subscribe to or read research-oriented journals, do not purchase theoretically and conceptually demanding text books or borrow them from libraries and do not attend staff development opportunities which have a research orientation. The personal libraries of early childhood professionals are more likely to be made up of popular literature on practical aspects of child development and psychology with some dated texts from pre-service training courses.

3   The inability of researchers to communicate research findings to practitioners—when early childhood professionals do read research reports, they complain that the theory, findings and recommendations are totally incomprehensible and therefore irrelevant. Because they lack training and skill in research methodology, the technical and abstract language of the researcher is difficult for the practitioner to understand and interpret. Researchers need to adapt the findings to the language of the practitioner to encourage their application. However, many researchers find this a difficult task given their limited familiarity with the practical contexts of early childhood services and would prefer to pursue their own research interests rather than become a translator for a group of professionals who do not appear receptive to what research has to offer.

Researchers tend to write for a specific audience, that is, other academics and colleagues in higher education. Academic journals in which most research is published are favoured by researchers because publication in such journals is related to career advancement. Such journals are not easily available to practitioners unless they are enrolled to study in higher education degrees. Other possible audiences, such as practitioners in the field, the general public, the press and media and policy makers at local and national levels, are perceived by many academic researchers to have less status compared to their colleagues.

4   Early childhood professionals tend to distrust research findings and new ideas and refuse to accept them often because they find personal security in the known and familiar. The decades of the 1960s and 1970s brought with them an attitude of 'change at any cost' which resulted in discontinuities in practice and subsequent suspicion about adopting innovations too quickly. Some practitioners are resistant to change and view change and innovation as unnecessary. Research findings alone are unlikely to stimulate change in established practices which have been derived from attitudes, values and beliefs that have been built up over many years.

5   The implementation of research findings and new ideas involves extra work for professionals who already have demanding jobs. Early childhood professionals who wish to implement the results of research may find it necessary to persuade committees of management or employers of cost-effective benefits, may need to devise new strategies and techniques and may need to clarify and restructure their value systems. All of this takes time and energy. Time is the most valuable but scarce resource for many early childhood practitioners who argue that this is the reason that they are not able to keep up with or implement new developments.

6   Early childhood professionals consider themselves to be autonomous and may use their traditional right to independence to justify poor practice. Some practitioners are suspicious that academic researchers (who are assumed to have little knowledge of and experience in working with young children and their families or who have been shut up in the academic ivory tower for so long that they have lost contact with the field) are trying to dictate what to do in early childhood services. Consequently, they choose to ignore the contribution that research can make. Lack of collaboration between researchers and practitioners has created an additional problem of 'ownership' where early childhood professionals are not involved in the production of research and therefore do not have a sense of 'ownership'. If this were gained through collaboration it could help to diminish any perceived threat to autonomy.

7   Early childhood professionals consider their work to be a practice-oriented art rather than a theoretically-based science. The dislike of theory, which is articulated throughout pre-service training, continues into workplace attitudes. Many practitioners find theory difficult to grasp because they have

not developed sophisticated conceptual and analytical skills. This cognitive limitation is linked to an inability to comprehend the relevance of theory to practice. They do not understand that theory and research are sources of knowledge which can be used as a guide to practice or as a resource, but alone are not sufficient to act as a foundation or directive for program design.

8 The present training programs and career structures for the early childhood field do not emphasise the skills of understanding, implementing and producing research as an integral aspect of professional leadership. The field needs more intelligent consumers of research as a basis for nurturing producers of research. However, unless early childhood professionals themselves take responsibility for extending the boundaries of knowledge and ideas in their own field, the present reliance on professionals outside the early childhood field to conduct research and shape its future will continue, a factor which will impede the budding professionalisation of the early childhood field.

The existence of the above obstacles to interest in and incorporation of research into decision making and change will not deter the effective early childhood leader who, while acknowledging these structural difficulties, will work towards overcoming them through the creation of a special ethos or atmosphere in the centre where research is valued for its contribution to the early childhood service and the professional learning and development of the staff.

Encouraging a research culture in the early childhood profession

There are many disincentives to consuming and producing research in the early childhood field. In order to address this problem, leadership needs to come from within the early childhood profession, from individuals who are innovative, flexible and creative and who combine these attributes with disciplined thinking based on accurate sources of information. Effective leaders need to make research and reflection an inherent part of their own activity and encourage their staff to do the same. One of the ways of elevating the status of research as a source of information for professional decision making and the initiation of change is by fostering a culture where research is valued.

What is a 'research culture'? It is really a matter of personal and professional attitude. It is also an environment in which intellectual interest and scientific curiosity exist and are evident. A research culture is a prevailing atmosphere, throughout the early childhood profession, at training and at service level, where individuals are motivated to seek additional knowledge which forms the basis of choices in practice whether they be by researcher, practitioner or parent. A research culture values theoretical and research-based knowledge which relates to child development and learning processes, interactional and instructional methods and human resource management.

There are a number of strategies which can be implemented to create and enhance a research culture in the early childhood profession which are described below.

- It should be acknowledged that the early childhood profession is a distinctive, unique profession which possesses its own traditions, values, assumptions, experiences, practices and training and is therefore capable of extending its own knowledge base without relying on other professionals to fulfil this role. A shift in attitude is necessary, that is, from one of deference to the opinions of experts and authorities from other professions to a healthy, questioning scepticism of the input from others and increasing respect for the contributions from members of the early childhood field.

- A greater acceptance of pluralism should be encouraged in the theoretical perspectives on which research is based. To date, research in early childhood has been based mainly on a psychological perspective, in particular developmental and educational psychology. In order to gain a deeper and broader understanding of the social reality of development, care and education, other perspectives, for example, sociology, ecology, biology, anthropology, history, philosophy, politics, curriculum theory and economics, need to become as familiar to early childhood practitioners as the psychological one. The early childhood field needs up-to-date information on a wide range of issues, problems and techniques to advance the provision of a range of quality services which will meet the needs of a changing society.

- A research orientation should be supported in training programs at all levels for students and staff so that research becomes an accepted and valued part of the professional culture. In this way, potential members of the field will have developed the skills to be intelligent consumers of research and to perceive their role as one which may include the production of research. In addition, encouraging practitioners to complete higher research-based degrees as part of their own staff development will begin to change the face of the field from a predominantly practice-oriented one to one in which there is a perceived balance between the scientific and practical needs required to meet the early childhood endeavour.

- Early childhood professionals should be encouraged to become involved in collaborative research. The gap between researcher and practitioner can be narrowed if more practitioners become involved in research, not only as post-graduate students but as equal partners in an interprofessional team in the research enterprise. The inclusion of practitioners in research teams can sensitise them to the entire research process in a way that promotes effective use of resources and improvement of practice. Collaborative investigations by researchers and practitioners should begin with a dialogue concerning values, beliefs, assumptions and local conditions in order to establish the basis of the research project. Individual responsibility, initiative and direction can be handled through responsible delegation by the team leader.

Collaborative research teams can overcome the problem and effects of lack of 'ownership' in the research endeavour. Lack of involvement in research can lead to important findings remaining unknown and consequently not being applied to appropriate circumstances by practitioners. Collaborative processes are a means of promoting communication and understanding between researcher and practitioner and help to ensure that research findings using a minimum of jargon are made available in simple and intelligent ways, so that they are easily understood by decision makers and consumers.

In their day-to-day practice, early childhood professionals are likely to possess intimate knowledge about and understanding of questions and problems which need to be addressed in a systematic investigation. Early childhood professionals can provide the clear link between real life issues and the needs of the field and the research questions which are defined for examination. The initiative should be taken to either undertake the necessary research themselves or to establish a collaborative, interdisciplinary team which includes practitioners and experienced researchers. While the research activities of developing, testing and confirming scientific knowledge are hardly pursuits that can be carried out in spare time at work, early childhood professionals need to be encouraged to engage in action research which can be conducted at a centre level.

• Research needs to be perceived as a routine problem solving exercise which can contribute to new knowledge and understanding as well as to practical outcomes.

These strategies will not change the prevailing culture of the early childhood profession overnight but an effective leader can signal the need for change in this area by focusing on the positive outcomes of valuing research as much as practice. The beginnings of a research culture in the early childhood field can be stimulated by a leader who supports staff to accept some responsibility for defining questions to be investigated by themselves or other researchers, for verifying research results reported in professional literature, and for ensuring cogent interpretation and practical application of relevant recommendations.

Action research as a guide to decision making and problem solving

Action research has been suggested as a means of professional development for those staff who are involved in education (Elliot, 1991) and as a way of helping bridge the gap between research and practice (Sigston, 1996). It is considered to enhance professional learning and to foster reflective practice. Several writers have asserted that educators and administrators would make better decisions and become more effective practitioners if they were willing and able to conduct action research in their places of work (Lieberman, 1956; Burton, 1986; Allen & Miller, 1990). Indeed, action research has been linked to quality improvement in the services provided for young children (Kelly, 1996; McNaughton, 1996). Early childhood professionals who are able to conduct this type of research in their centres are able to demonstrate creative leadership in their ability to diagnose and respond to problems and the need for change in a systematic manner. Action research has been suggested as a vehicle for increasing professionalism because, through the process of conducting action research, practitioners begin to value research and develop a professional culture that values reflection (Whitford et al., 1987).

The term 'action research' refers to a way of thinking that uses reflection and inquiry as a way of understanding the conditions that support or inhibit change, the nature of change, the process of change and the results of the attempt to change (Clift et al., 1990). Action research entails action disciplined by inquiry and combines the research procedure with a substantive act (Hopkins, 1990). The goal is to improve practice which is an ongoing concern for all members of the early childhood profession. In order to optimise a successful outcome for action research undertaken by early childhood professionals, the problems chosen to be explored need to be significant for the leader and the team in terms of the mission, objectives and quality of the service. The problems must be manageable within a realistic time frame and appropriate for the research skills of the people involved. A healthy attitude within the team to problem solving, risk taking and experimentation is also helpful and needs to be tempered by the leader with realistic expectations about the unpredictability of change and the probability of immediate success.

Wadsworth (1997) and Kemmis and McTaggert (1988) give clear, practical descriptions of action research for human service professionals. The following steps briefly outline the action research process and cycle.

1 Identifying problems of mutual concern—The present problems are brought into focus through the processes of observation and reflection by all members of the team.
2 Analysing problems and determining possible contributing factors—The ability to diagnose the determinants of a problem is required. The existing situation is monitored using recorded, uncensored and uninterpreted observations from members of the team.
3 Forming tentative working hypotheses or guesses to explain these factors—At this point, questionable assumptions are eliminated. Decisions are made about the form and method of interpretation of the data which are to be collected.
4 Collecting and interpreting data from observations, interviews and relevant documents to clarify these hypotheses and to develop action hypotheses—Accurate details of events need to be recorded in order to avoid erroneous or superficial influences.

5   Formulating plans for action and carrying them out—Plans are experimental, prospective and forward-looking and may involve the acquisition of new skills or procedures in order to implement the plans.

6   Evaluating the results of the action—The processes of observation and reflection are used to critically assess the effects of the informed action and to make sense of the processes and issues that unfolded during the implementation phase. Collaborative reflection provides an opportunity to reconstruct meaning out of the situation and establishes the basis for a revised plan.

7   Introducing a revised cycle from Step 1 to Step 6.

Because becoming engaged in action research can be perceived as yet another role and responsibility to take on, and another demand on the already heavy work load of early childhood professionals, it is important that some non-research related considerations be highlighted. Although some early childhood professionals initiate projects that could be called action research, these are often abandoned for a range of reasons (Webb, 1996). It appears that recognition by would-be researchers of the importance of other factors in the success of action research projects is an essential aspect. Borgia and Schuler (1996) outline what they call 'The 5 Cs of Action Research' which refer to some other important components related to successful action research. They argue that involvement in action research includes the following components:

1   Commitment (giving and taking time, developing trust with participants)

2   Collaboration (sharing, giving, taking, listening, reflection, respect)

3   Concern (developing a support group of critical friends, risk taking)

4   Consideration (reflection about and critical assessment of one's professional actions)

5   Change (working towards growth, development and improvement in a nurturing, supportive environment)

Without support, encouragement and commitment from colleagues and research project participants, undertaking action research can be a threatening and demoralising experience. It is the interpersonal aspect of action research which makes it particularly relevant for early childhood practitioners, given the philosophical focus on the importance of positive and constructive interpersonal communication and relationships for all of the children and adults who are concerned with early care and education services.

Although some academic researchers regard action research conducted by other professionals (for example, early childhood practitioners) in their own environments as deficient in sound methodology and competent research skills, there is little doubt that skill in action research can contribute to improvements in practice and raise the critical consciousness of those involved. One of the major benefits flowing out of action research is enhanced staff professional development because of the focus on practitioner learning (Allen & Miller, 1990). In accepting the responsibility to systematically research solutions to common problems and goals, mutual respect and teamwork can be enhanced. Action research provides another opportunity where professional leadership can be demonstrated by any member of the team. However, the designated leader retains the major responsibility for convincing the team of the necessity for and usefulness of action research as a means of problem solving and responding to the need for change.

One final aspect related to undertaking action research or indeed any type of research is awareness of and adherence to the ethical principles underpinning research involving children and adults. Those conducting research need to appreciate their moral obligations to those participating in or affected by any research project and strike a balance between the pursuit of knowledge and understanding and the rights of children and adults who are included in the project. Cohen and Manion (1994) suggest that ethical issues in research can stem from a range of issues, including the nature of the specific issue under investigation, the context, research procedures, data collection methods and the uses of data. The following principles are in general use in academic research departments and provide guidelines for would-be researchers about the kinds of ethical considerations which need to be addressed before beginning any research project.

- Informed consent: Participants should be made aware of the focus of the research and any features of the research which might affect their decision to take part in the project. In the case of children, informed consent should be obtained from parents or adults who act *in loco parentis.*
- Openness and honesty: Participants should be made aware of

the specific purpose of the research. Deception is regarded as unacceptable, unprofessional and unethical behaviour.

- Right to withdraw: Participants should be informed at the beginning of the study that they may withdraw at any time and may choose not to engage in specific aspects of the study, answer specific questions or provide specific information.
- Protection from harm: Participants must be protected from experiencing physical or psychological harm during the project. While it is unlikely that early childhood research would result in physical harm, some research may focus upon sensitive or delicate issues which participants may find stressful. Researchers have an obligation to minimise stress arising out of research projects and to provide support to alleviate such stress.
- Debriefing: Participants have a right to have access to oral or written information about the procedures, processes and results following the conclusion of any research that they participate in.
- Confidentiality: Unless participants give specific consent regarding identification, researchers must ensure that confidentiality of identity of individuals and organisations is maintained during the project and in any ensuing publications.
- Ethical principles of professional bodies: Where professional bodies, such as the Australian Early Childhood Association or the Australian Psychological Society, have published their own guidelines and principles, these must be consulted and adhered to in the design and conduct of any research project.

The above principles are designed to protect both participants and researchers from potentially difficult situations which can arise in undertaking research. Early childhood professionals who wish to become involved in research are encouraged to develop, interpret and extend such considerations as are appropriate for early childhood settings.

To conclude, research activity is an effective way for early childhood practitioners to improve the quality of their services and to shape their image and reputation. Continued professionalisation of the early childhood field requires a revitalisation of the knowledge base (Silin, 1988) and the rationality and justice of practice. Some would go so far as to argue for a total reconceptualisation of the early childhood field. Early childhood professionals need to establish their own research base (Caldwell, 1984) which reflects a balanced interdisciplinary inquiry by practitioners within the field into theoretical and practical concerns. In addition to fostering a positive attitude to research by encouraging a research culture, the early childhood profession could elevate the status of research in Australia by the establishment of a clearing house which would centralise research findings so that they are more accessible for practitioners (Rodd, 1990). While it is acknowledged that research is a slow but effective tool for change and progress, early childhood professionals need to acquire knowledge about and skill in research technology so that they can command sufficient authority and respect to play a central role in the professionalisation of their own field.

8

A partnership with parents and the public

In the past decade, the early childhood field has been undergoing enormous change in a range of areas which has left many early childhood professionals with a sense of uncertainty about their future role in the community. The field is likely to remain in a state of flux until some agreement is reached between members of the field, academic training staff, government regulating bodies and unions about the models of care and education which best meet the needs of children and the community, minimum mandatory qualifications and associated awards (which may help eliminate many of the current inequities in the staffing of early childhood centres) and the roles and responsibilities that early childhood professionals are expected to undertake. As long as the early childhood field is perceived to lack clear direction in the current debate over its future, public support cannot be expected. Early childhood professionals themselves will need to be more politically active in articulating their views and concerns in order to help shape their own destiny.

In the past, early childhood professionals have happily accepted government action on behalf of children and families (Kagan, 1988). Yet, when government policies failed to reflect the experience and opinions of the early childhood field, some ambivalence about where the actual responsibility for policies and planning began to be encountered. The onus for representing the views and desires of the early childhood field in terms of the appropriate use of their expertise in the community must be taken up by the present leaders of early childhood centres. These people are the public face of early childhood, responsible for public relations with the range of people that they come across in their position including parents, other professionals and the general public (Curry, 1989; Hostetler, 1991). Because community understanding about the type of high-level skills which are required to fulfil the complexities of the early childhood professional role is clearly linked to professional recognition by the community, it is essential that leaders consider how they will fulfil this aspect of their leadership role. Early childhood professionals need to perceive parents as allies rather than adversaries. Parents, through their contact with and involvement in early childhood centres, can provide feedback and information that assists in enhancing community understanding of the roles and responsibilities which are associated with working in these centres (Goffin, 1988). Helping parents understand the early childhood profession's vision and objectives is the first step towards increasing public awareness of and eventually support for early childhood services.

Working with parents as partners in the early childhood team

In Australia, as in Britain and America, one of the significant changes that has occurred recently in the role of the early childhood professional has been with regard to community expectations and demand for increasing parent involvement in the operation of centres. Parents and programs for parents have been a part of the early childhood movement since the 1920s (Finkelstein, 1988) where periodic interest has been shown by early childhood professionals in themes of partnership (that is, a philosophy of shared child rearing), continuity (that is, the promotion of consistency between the conditions and experience of centre and home) and parent education (that is, the professional responsibility to support and educate parents to enhance children's well-being and parental enjoyment and competence in the parenting role (Powell, 1989)). Although not new in focus, the current resurgence of interest by early childhood professionals in helping parents to understand their children and the parenting role in ways that are advantageous to them both signifies a move towards a holistic approach to professional practice with children and families and an affirmation of the traditional role in programmatic work with families. This additional responsibility for parents as well as

163

children underlines a marked shift in roles which has taken place over the past decade for early childhood professionals.

Parental involvement in early childhood programs has been regarded by many experts in the early childhood field as a crucial element in the provision of quality programs (Galinsky, 1990; Shimoni, 1991; Henry, 1996; Rennie, 1996). However, it is perceived to be a source of tension and one of the most difficult aspects of the early childhood professional's role (Powell, 1989; Galinsky, 1990). Research findings which demonstrate the beneficial connection between parental participation in programs and children's achievement in educational settings (Henderson, 1987; Greenberg, 1989) have been available for professionals since the 1960s (Galen, 1991). Although parental participation in early childhood services has been increasingly encouraged over the past thirty years, such research evidence is a compelling argument for strengthening parental involvement, from the typically token level to a level of genuine partnership, in any service related to the care and education of young children. In addition to benefits for children, parents' involvement as members of the early childhood team means that they can act as advocates for early childhood services. Early childhood professionals who include parents in genuine decision making in the centre have taken a political step towards initiating innovative change in the early childhood field.

Early childhood professionals have historically defined their client group broadly (Peters, 1988b) and have considered their relationship with parents as an added dimension to their practice (Mitchell, 1989). Educators have long recognised the significant influence of the family on the care and education of young children and have attempted to support parents in their own growth and development (Anastasiow, 1988). Parents are a group of people who could be regarded as 'secondary clients' with their children being the early childhood professional's 'primary clients' (Katz, 1988). Given that it is the goal of every professional educator to assist the client to achieve more meaningful experience in her life (Katz, 1988), the potential for early childhood professionals to demonstrate leadership in work with parents as a secondary client group is high. Yet, little specialised training has been provided for practitioners to work with the adults, either parents or staff members (Jorde-Bloom, 1992; Honig, 1996) who make up the team within an early childhood centre. This is likely to account for some of the frustration that early childhood professionals experience in this role.

What is parent involvement in early childhood centres?

Part of the difficulty of involving parents in early childhood centres revolves around the apparent confusion among early childhood professionals about what the term actually signifies. While early childhood professionals have always involved parents in some capacity, usually at a token level, they have generally retained their traditional autonomy (Almy, 1988). However, over the past thirty years, differing attitudes and beliefs have dictated that closer and more meaningful links between parent and professional be established. While the prevailing philosophies have changed with the times, they have initiated changes in the relationship between parent and professional, some of which have been adopted willingly while others have sparked some resistance.

Demand for parental involvement at more than a token level, such as providing an extra pair of hands in the centre, arose in the 1960s when governments in Western societies focused on the idea that democracy should be extended beyond politics and formal government in the lives of ordinary people to include '. . . maximum, feasible participation . . .' (Powell, 1989:5) in decision making by those affected by the ultimate decision. Early childhood professionals have been slow to incorporate the full spirit of the partnership approach to working with parents because they have clung to the belief that they are the experts when it comes to children and early childhood services. This has resulted in a slow process of change where early childhood professionals first took a compensatory approach to parental involvement in which deficit models of family life were responded to with the provision of interventionist strategies (Cohen, 1988). Parents tended to be perceived by early childhood professionals as being deficient in parenting capability, that is, not possessing the knowledge and skills to create a family environment in which to properly raise their children. Early childhood professionals considered themselves as appropriately qualified and experienced mediators to compensate for perceived parental shortfalls in relation to children. Some parent education programs still reflect a compensatory approach where early childhood professionals, who erroneously believe that they are the experts when it comes to children and families, attempt to change 'dysfunctional families' into 'successful families'.

The 1970s saw a new philosophy which convinced early childhood professionals that they could enhance their professionalism in the eyes of parents by improving communication and developing positive relationships. The catchcry of the day was 'informed interest' where it was believed that parental involvement was a matter of communication and contact. Any sense of parental alienation from the centre that the child was attending was thought to be overcome by providing information about what and how well the child was doing at the centre. The philosophy of communication gave way to the philosophy of accountability in the 1980s where parents began to be perceived as consumers of a service who possessed rights and responsibilities which early childhood professionals were obliged to meet. Parents tended to be regarded as a 'market with needs and wants' to whom professionals needed to be sensitive and responsive. Parental involvement at this level found early childhood professionals consulting and discussing policies, procedures and practices with parents or their committee representatives but little real partnership or collaboration.

In the report of a review of early childhood services in the state of Victoria (Report, 1983), parents' rights to have control over decisions which affect the lives of their children were clearly affirmed. It was recommended that early childhood services be planned to facilitate effective participation by and accountability to parents. Effective participation was defined as 'active management' of services, rather than expression of opinion which was regarded as tokenism. It was argued that the management structures of early childhood services should reflect the partnership approach between parents, professionals and other staff. This nascent partnership orientation was revealed in an official statement of the goals of The Lady Gowrie Child Care Centre, Brisbane (Watts & Patterson, 1984) where priority was given to providing services which encouraged liaison, involvement and the sharing of responsibility for child rearing between home and centre.

The push towards the adoption of a true philosophy of partnership has begun to gather momentum in the 1990s with early childhood professionals finally recognising that they have both shared and complementary goals with the parents who are associated with their centre. Early childhood professionals are beginning to accept that both parents and professionals are experts when it comes to children and families but that they each bring different types of expertise. This shift to a partnership approach emphasises the impact that both home and centre have on young children and the need to coordinate the efforts of parents and professionals through non-hierarchical, collaborative relationships. The willingness of early childhood professionals to share power and responsibility with parents in a partnership of equals is another illustration of team leadership to achieve the centre's mission and objectives.

The partnership approach to parent involvement stresses co-operative rather than joint activity and permits parents to decide upon the level of involvement which is appropriate in terms of their priorities and commitments. Wolfendale (1996) argues that such an approach to parent involvement stems from an ideological perspective where working relationships are based on and valued by equal but different contributions from and shared accountability of parents and professionals. Wolfendale (1983) suggests that professionals who engage in a partnership approach to parental involvement do so on the basis of the following premises (Cohen, 1988:5–6):

- parents are experts on their own children;
- parental skills complement those of the professional;
- parents can make informed observations and impart vital information to professionals;
- parents have the right to be involved;
- parents should contribute to decision making; and
- parents can be highly effective teachers of their own children.

The following characteristics have been ascribed by Wolfendale (1986) to parents who are perceived by professionals as partners in rather than consumers of children's services:

- parents exhibit different but equal strengths and equivalent expertise;
- parents contribute to as well as receive services;
- parents are active and central in decision making; and
- parents share responsibility and accountability with professionals.

These premises and characteristics are useful guidelines for early childhood professionals who wish to establish a collaborative relationship with parents or who wish to assess the extent to which their relationship with and involvement of parents is that of a partnership. Powell (1989) outlined a range of activities that are suitable for creating parent partnership involvement and contribution. A range of strategies for promoting a partnership with parents exist which include inviting parents to:

- attend and participate in staff meetings to assist, for example, in reviewing and making decisions about early childhood philosophy, goals, policies, standards, expectations, curricula and programs;

- work in conjunction with an experienced staff member on special skill development projects with their own or other children;
- develop activities related to parent-initiated needs and interests, such as parent education programs;
- volunteer their expertise for special program activities, such as in music, movement, stories and multicultural perspectives;
- contribute to criteria for and the process of staff selection; and
- contribute to reviewing centre budgets and fund-raising.

Where however does this partnership approach leave the early childhood professional? How can professional expertise be used? What is your professional standing with colleagues, peers, other professionals and the community when partnership means that you are mutually responsible and accountable with a person who is also a consumer and a secondary client of the centre? Could professional efforts to maximise parental involvement and influence undermine the leader's efforts to achieve the early childhood centre's mission and objectives for implementing culturally and developmentally-appropriate programs and practice according to the values and beliefs of the profession?

Research suggests that parents' ideas about how children develop and learn are by no means clear or straightforward (Cohen, 1988). Parents, like early childhood professionals, have their own widely differing implicit theories about children (Goodnow & Collins, 1990). Parental theories have been constructed largely from their own family of origin experiences and as they have lived with and cared for their own children. Early childhood professionals have developed their own theories on the basis of their own experience in a similar way to parents but usually have interpreted this experience in the light of knowledge and skills gained during training and the experience of working with large numbers of children in a variety of settings. Parental theories and professional theories about what is the right way to work with children leads then to differing perspectives on policies, procedures and practice. The early childhood professional needs to bring all her expertise to finding a common ground between the two perspectives.

The answer to the dilemma of finding a pathway to partnership with parents is to negotiate a cooperative agreement concerning the planning and implementation of the early childhood program. In this way, the professional accepts the responsibility to meet other people's needs (that is, those of the parents) by making their expertise available to the parents for their consideration. The early childhood professional also meets her own needs by recognising the value of training, experience and philosophy as information sources for making decisions about how, when and where young children's development and learning can be facilitated. The leader who effectively creates a partnership with parents in early childhood services possesses the confidence to articulate her philosophy concerning care and early education while simultaneously acknowledging parental rights, information, theories, expectations, problems and pressures.

In this way, the perceived complementary expertise of both parent and professional can be brought to meet the needs of the situation in mutually agreed ways. Davis (1985) suggests that the early childhood professional's role is to encourage dialogue with parents about alternative perspectives on children's development and learning and to point out different ways of responding to or intervening in issues related to care and education. The success of this approach will depend on the early childhood professional's skills to communicate with the parents. The effectiveness of how the information is imparted entails the ability to:

- clearly and unambiguously explain issues in an egalitarian as opposed to a paternalistic style;
- remain non-judgemental and overcome stereotyped and/or prejudiced attitudes in interaction;
- listen with understanding to parents' views and acknowledge their feelings;
- respond in a way that will enhance the perception of team spirit and relationship;
- respond professionally where personal feelings are managed and expressed appropriately;
- confidently assert one's professional opinion;
- recognise and respond to conflict appropriately; and
- involve parents as active and equal members of the decision making team.

Obstacles to partnerships with parents

Developing skills to work effectively in partnership with parents takes time and experience. Lack of time, for both parents and professionals, is a big obstacle to building the respectful relationship that is required in a partnership. Given that relatively little formal training has been available for developing skills related to this aspect of early childhood practice, it is not surprising to find that some early childhood professionals give perfunctory recognition to this extra responsibility.

Katz (1977; 1995a) and Vander Ven (1988) have identified the fact that the type of relationship developed with parents and the level of parental involvement in early childhood centres appears to be determined by the stage of professional development that a leader has achieved. Vander Ven suggests that it is not until Stage 3—Informed Practice, when practitioners have made a strong career commitment to the early childhood field, that they develop the awareness of the necessity for working collaboratively with parents. For Katz, it is not until practitioners have reached the Consolidation stage that they are able to begin to respond to parental needs and expectations concerning the program. A shift in maturity as well as a broader perspective is considered to be the stimulus for identification with parents and families as well as children. At earlier stages of career development and professional maturity, relationships with parents are more likely to be author-itarian and paternalistic, token in nature and from a deficit perspective, that is, where parents, even those who are consider-ably older than the staff member, are not thought to possess the knowledge and skills necessary for bringing up their children. This approach is unlikely to empower parents to develop skill and competence in their own lives.

One of the effects of parents' lack of professional knowledge in terms of their involvement in early childhood centres is that practitioners may implement forms of support and opportunities for involvement which do not match parental needs, expectations and characteristics. The initiation of any change in an early childhood program should be on the basis of diagnosed need, which has been discussed in Chapter 7. Effective leadership of parents entails understanding parental needs in order to tailor programs which are related to particular stages of parenthood (Galinsky, 1981), specific needs expressed by parents, and the social and cultural characteristics of parents as well as parents' levels of educational achievement (Powell & Stremmel, 1987). Any dimension of practice with parents should be subject to a process of objective evaluation to ensure that both the processes and the outcomes are appropriate for the parents. Research evidence has demonstrated that some undesirable but unintentional results can flow out of poorly designed and implemented experiences for parents (Hess, 1980). There is little point in putting energy into parent support, resourcing, education or partnership if it is not what the particular group of parents want. Early childhood professionals should provide parent programs that meet parents' expressed or objectively assessed needs and not rely on their subjective perception of their role in relation to parents.

If early childhood professionals wish to define parents as members of the team which provides quality care and education for young children, the way in which parents are involved needs to be collaborative in nature. A reciprocal relationship, such as in a partnership, can ensure that the staff and the program of an early childhood centre are sensitive and responsive to the needs and norms of the children and parents who use the centre. However, both parents and early childhood professionals need assistance to understand the parameters of their respective roles as they begin to explore the effects of the equal balance of power in the partnership (Powell, 1989). Collaborative parent–professional relationships can be the starting point for growth and change in parents, early childhood professionals and the programs they offer. As Shimoni (1991) points out, of all the groups that early childhood professionals interact with, it is parents who will play the leading role in determining the recognition of the professional status of the early childhood field.

Leadership in the public domain

To this point, leadership has been discussed in the context of interaction with the staff and parents who are associated with an early childhood centre, with leadership effectiveness being evaluated in terms of child well-being, goal attainment related to program responsiveness, and adult morale and personal development. Little reference has been made to leadership activities outside the centre in the public domain. However, this aspect of leadership cannot be ignored because of the pressing need to develop and exercise leadership at the grass roots level. In other professions, leadership usually is defined as an integral aspect of organisational sustainability and is evaluated in terms of its effectiveness both within the organisation and within the external environment in which the organisation operates. Once early childhood professionals are encouraged to extend their concern beyond the direct care of children, they can move to a position where they can begin to use their communication skills to champion the rights of children and adults in early childhood centres in the wider context (Almy, 1985). The leadership activities which are relevant for the wider external environment in which early childhood services operate are addressed below.

In general terms, leadership activities which are related to the broader context can be described as advocacy (Simons, 1986). Advocacy has been a term which has been used in the early childhood field to stimulate practitioners' perception of their personal responsibility for raising the profile of children and families and the early childhood profession in the eyes of the community (Goffin & Lombardi, 1988). However, it appears that the term 'advocacy' is not clearly or widely understood by members of the early childhood field. The word 'advocacy' tends to conjure up images of politics and protest for many early childhood professionals who have yet to understand and identify with the political element of their role. Becoming politically aware simply entails understanding how the policies of the public and private sectors affect the lives of children, families and the early childhood profession.

Responding to that understanding with committed action is the first step towards demonstrating the political dimension of leadership. With early childhood services constantly under the threat of closure, restriction and withdrawal of funding it appears that survival may depend on the abilities of some members of the field to engage in those activities, called leadership or advocacy, which will bring key issues to a wide audience (Ebbeck, 1990).

Once early childhood professionals understand that advocacy is merely a shorthand term for bringing professional leadership knowledge and skills to benefit children, families and the early childhood profession, they can begin to engage in some of the wide range of activities that are required to enhance the status of children and families and the professionalisation of the field. This must be understood as a long and slow process of change which will require high levels of self-confidence and assertive ability to overcome the obstacles and setbacks to initiating change. Activities which are related to this dimension of leadership are participation in professional organisations, research and writing, networking with other professionals and becoming political and using the media. These activities take time, effort and the development of special knowledge and skills in order to become influential in the arenas which have the power to make decisions and change policy. While advocacy is the responsibility of every member of the early childhood field (Caldwell, 1984; Pascal, 1992; Rodd, 1997a), it is a particular responsibility of the leader because she will have a broader perspective of the current needs in the early childhood field.

Collaboration with other relevant professional organisations has been recommended as one way to solve the complex problems in early childhood service provision (Ellison & Barbour, 1992). The literature suggests that bringing members from organisations concerned with advocating for children and families may facilitate systematic problem solving which appears to be difficult for one group alone. For, example, bringing together members from child-care and teaching, or from private and public child-care organisations, who share similar concerns about services for children seems logical, desirable and time efficient. Collaborative activity requires that participants share mutual aspirations, a common conceptual framework, agreed goals and agreed out-comes of the project. To be an effective collaboration, responsi-bility must be delegated and control shared (Hord, 1986).

Collaboration with other professional groups is a means rather than an end in terms of addressing issues in early childhood care and education. A united collaborative multiprofessional group can speak with more weight and command more respect from the decision makers than one organisation alone. It is an effective means of using the knowledge, expertise and perspectives of the individuals with a variety of backgrounds who make up the early childhood field as well as a way of encouraging them to take responsibility for and to contribute to policy making and planning issues.

Participation in professional organisations

As a leader, it is important not only to join but to become active in the organisations which are concerned with early childhood services. With the literature, seminars and conferences offered by professional organisations, such as The Australian Early Childhood Association, The Australian Association of Early Childhood Educa-tors and The Kindergarten Teachers Association, opportunities are provided for continued professional development. They are also an arena where problems or issues which are of concern to early childhood professionals are identified, discussed and responded to. Professional organisations are often the vehicles by which groups of practitioners bring issues of concern to the attention of the wider early childhood field, parents, unions, politicians, business and the media. However, they rely upon the efforts of their membership to be effective. The larger the number of people whose views are represented by the organisation, the stronger and more effective will be the impact of their actions.

As well as professional associations and unions, there are advisory boards, committees and working parties at local, state and national level where an early childhood member can be influential in accomplishing change. By becoming a member of one of these organisations, individuals can represent the perspective of the early childhood field. Such organisations provide direct access to influencing decision making and change (Goffin & Lombardi, 1988).

In addition, membership of professional organisations enlarges the opportunity for professional contact with colleagues. This is an important function given the isolation that most early childhood professionals work in. Those in positions of leadership often complain that they have less access to support in their centre than other members of the team because of the need to keep some distance from staff in order to retain authority. In addition, the narrower perspective of team members compared with that of the leader means that team members are unable to empathise with the leader. Contact with colleagues who are able to understand the leader's position and provide the emotional support that may not be available at centre level is available through membership of professional organisations and is a way of initiating and building a support network.

Research and writing

The role and advantages of research as a source of information for decision making and change have been discussed in Chapter 7. However, research is also important for leadership in the public domain because it is a recognised means of gathering the facts and information which carry weight in arguments for change. The use of research findings gives substance and credibility to an issue (Goffin & Lombardi, 1988) and helps decision makers focus on the key issues and consider different alternatives (Glass, 1987).

Professional organisations usually have a research interest and can provide support for and access to relevant research findings. However, as has been stated previously in Chapter 7, it is not sufficient to be a consumer of other people's research. Leadership requires that commitment be made to produce research which has been initiated from the early childhood professional's intimate knowledge of the current needs and concerns of the field.

The next step is to disseminate research findings, ideas and concerns in ways which will reach and be understood by the intended audience. Something as simple as the leader writing her concerns about an issue in the centre's newsletter is a way of informing parents and activating their interest in supporting continued effort to address the issue. Writing letters to politicians, government ministers and the editors of newspapers and magazines is another way of providing leadership on behalf of children, families and the profession. Publication in a professional journal requires greater effort and skill which may need to be acquired through further study but it is not outside the capabilities of many early childhood professionals. The real purpose of writing is to express an informed opinion on a critical issue in clear, understandable and accurate ways.

Whereas writing can be done during or outside work hours, speaking, the alternative means of communicating a point of view, requires specific time commitments usually away from the centre. This may be more difficult for early childhood professionals who are required to maintain strict child:staff ratios during working hours and who may find the extra demands on their personal time too burdensome. However, this activity should not be avoided. Opportunities to express a point of view arise informally with parents, staff, colleagues, members of the local neighbourhood and community, friends and formally at meetings, seminars and conferences and with employers. Speaking formally or informally is another way of informing others and building support for an issue and should not be overlooked by the early childhood professional.

Networking with other professionals

Leaders who act as advocates on behalf of the early childhood profession need the support of others, such as parents, the general public, politicians and administrators to help them achieve their goals. However, achievement of goals is likely to be more efficient if the leader engages the support of and acts in collaboration with members of other professional groups who have an interest in early childhood (Almy, 1988). Change can be accomplished more effectively if it is supported by a range of professional groups rather than appearing to be the concern of a single professional group (Ellison & Barbour, 1992). Networking with colleagues from related professions gives access to a greater range of knowledge and skill which can strengthen the weight of any argument. Moral support, encouragement and feedback can also be provided by colleagues outside the early childhood profession (Goffin & Lombardi, 1988), which can help strengthen the resolve and commitment essential to pursue the issue of concern.

Networks can be informal where individuals with common interests and goals link up to share information and to plan action on a regular basis. They can also be formal networks where committees or working parties are formed with official representation from professional organisations, institutions or agencies. The advantages of establishing and participating in a network system are that isolation is broken down, awareness of others' interests and activities is increased, barriers to communication are decreased and misunderstanding and miscommunication is diminished. Successful networking takes time. Early childhood professionals will require all their skills in communication and interpersonal relationships to build the cooperation of others.

The strength of networking is in the development of trusting relationships where allies and supporters can be called upon when required to add impact to activity. Early childhood professionals who establish strong networks with colleagues from other professions can encourage these other professionals to assist in raising the status of early childhood in the community. Networking is another way of reaching out to the community to enhance understanding of and enlarge support for the early childhood profession's vision, mission, goals and concerns (Levine, 1992).

Becoming political and using the media

For too long, the early childhood profession has maintained that children and politics do not mix (Simons, 1986). The failure to perceive the connection between early childhood services and politics accounts in part for the slow and extended process of professionalisation in the field today. While early childhood professionals have acted as advocates for children and families (Almy, 1988), their narrow conceptualisation of the role of power in politics and their unwillingness to become involved in the political arena has meant that their achievements are probably far lower than was possible potentially. Steering clear of politics has kept the status of the early childhood profession low (Simons, 1986). A report on the future directions and strategies of teacher education in Australia (*Teacher Education: Directions and Strategies*, 1990) pointed out that in order to meet the challenges of most early childhood career opportunities in a changing society, the early childhood professional would need to be politically aware. Proficiency in direct care and teaching, personnel management and administration will no longer be sufficient.

Moving away from the traditional apolitical stance (Silin, 1988) to becoming politically aware and active is likely to produce a number of benefits for the early childhood field. Firstly, it informs the government about the needs and requirements of children and families. Secondly, it explains the crucial role that early childhood professionals play in promoting child and family welfare. Thirdly, it signals issues which are emerging as important concerns for those who are responsible for supporting children and families in the society. However, it is unlikely that early childhood professionals who have not reached Stage 4—Complex or Stage 5—Influential in their professional career development (Vander Ven, 1988) will have gained sufficient intellectual independence to produce the kind of proactive orientation which is required to become politically active and influential.

Becoming political entails understanding the process of democratic government and legislature, knowing who the local, state and federal representatives are in government and their platforms on issues of concern to early childhood professionals, knowing who their counterparts are, being able to identify the public servants who administer the government department(s) responsible for early childhood services and being prepared to lobby by expressing an opinion personally or in writing to the appropriate government official.

Lobbying is the process of informing public officials and others relevant about the issues which confront early childhood professionals on a daily basis. Wilkins and Blank (1986) define it as 'getting the right information to the right person at the right time'. If politicians and government officials are ignorant of the issues,

177

they are unlikely to take any action. There are many other groups with loud voices and well-organised campaigns who will capture the attention of the policy and decision makers in government. If they are only part informed or misinformed, they cannot be expected to make decisions which will be perceived as appropriate by those who are better informed on the subject of early childhood.

Persistence in attempting to make meaningful contact with public officials is essential. Those who are easily fobbed off will make little progress in getting a hearing. The long history of reticence by early childhood professionals to speak out and articulate their contribution and concerns has meant that a weak basis of power, if it exists at all, is the starting point for attempts to influence the actions of public officials on behalf of children, families and early childhood staff. Given that early childhood professionals have a long way to go in becoming politically powerful, Goffin and Lombardi (1988) suggest that one of the best ways of gaining the support of public officials is to invite them to the early childhood centre and begin to establish a personal relationship with them. In this way, the early childhood professional will come to be perceived as a community expert on early childhood issues and her opinions will have more influence on government decisions.

Becoming involved politically means becoming involved in the decision-making process on issues which affect children, families and the early childhood profession. It means perceiving the political dimension in early childhood issues and acting in ways which will ensure that issues in early childhood command greater attention and priority within the community.

The media are increasingly powerful tools which can be used to shape public opinion in our society. Most people, especially women, are interested in news related to children and families, especially in the local community. Many media reporters are interested in the issues which are of concern to early childhood professionals because these are topical issues which capture people's attention. However, the media continue to be under-utilised by early childhood professionals as a means of disseminating information and opinion to the public. In addition to providing information, Simons (1986) suggests that 'pointing out the other side' to comment which is critical of children's services is an equally important responsibility of early childhood professionals. Regardless of the format chosen, such as a letter to the editor, a short article focusing on a particular issue for the local newspaper or an interview for television or radio, the early childhood professional needs to focus on using the media to keep issues in front of the public eye and to build up community awareness.

In conclusion, early childhood professionals can increase the status of children, families and the field if they define part of their leadership role as reaching out to the community. The way in which contact with the local, state, federal and even international communities is made can take a variety of forms, from working with parents, other professionals and accessing all the available channels of communication. Continued efforts by early childhood professionals within the community can foster change in awareness and understanding about the fundamental importance of and the vital role played by early childhood services which will eventually benefit children and families and move the field along the pathway of increased professionalism.

9

The ethics of leadership

The changing world of leadership has forced the adoption of new perceptions about and understandings of this phenomenon by professionals in many fields, including early childhood care and education. The relationship between leadership, quality and organisational effectiveness has been well documented throughout this book. For those of us working with young children and their families, leadership has been recognised as possessing caring, educational and more recently moral aspects. Previous chapters in this book have explored some of the caring and educational aspects of leadership. However, little reference has been made to the moral aspects of leadership in early childhood with the exception of the role of a code of ethics in guiding decision making. It is important now to recognise the inter-relationship between these three aspects of leadership. An effective leader, particularly one who is intimately involved and influential in the lives and welfare of children and families, needs to understand the impact of who they are, how they behave and their decisions on people's lives. The continued professionalisation of the early childhood field is dependent upon members of the field understanding and accepting that they have a responsibility to become politically aware and to act as advocates for children and families (Rodd, 1997a).

In attempting to explain the moral aspect of leadership, some authors have likened the leader to a high priest or priestess. Ripley (1994) described the leader's role as one of influencing the followers to accept and adopt the values and beliefs, vision and the virtues espoused by the organisational ethos. While the terminology Ripley used to describe the leader may be flamboyant, few early childhood professionals would disagree with the inclusion of a moral aspect in their definition of leadership. Indeed, many would agree that leadership can be understood as a moral act which is guided by personal and professional values and principles about what is right and wrong and in the best interests of individuals and groups.

In early childhood, leaders are considered to hold social responsibility for enhancing the potential of the children and adults with whom they interact (Perreault, 1991) and protecting their welfare, for laying the foundations for life long learning (Page, 1995) and for providing quality services which are relevant and responsive to the communities they serve (Pugh, 1996). They are charged with a moral responsibility to act as advocates for children, families and the profession (Pascal, 1992), that is to be articulate, organised and skilful in acting as a voice for individuals and groups who may be vulnerable and powerless.

In relation to the moral or ethical aspect of effective leadership in early childhood, four key areas need to be considered. These are:

1 the promotion and protection of children's rights;
2 the provision of a quality and economically viable service which does not compromise children's rights;
3 the administration of a centre in accordance with the profession's ethical principles; and
4 the employment of an early childhood code of ethics to guide the resolution of ethical dilemmas.

The understanding about, reflection on and resultant decisions related to such areas can produce leadership that corresponds to ethical practice in early childhood settings. These areas are considered to be part of the ethical domain because they are related to '. . . ideas about how people ought to behave, how people ought to treat one another, and what obligations people have to one another' (Mulligan, 1996:102). The implications of each of these areas in the ethics of leadership for early childhood professionals will be discussed.

Promoting and protecting children's rights

One of the primary and significant responsibilities of any adult but especially leaders in early childhood centres is to make decisions and act in ways that promote and protect the rights of young children who generally are considered to be dependent, vulnerable and voiceless in contemporary society. Rayner (1995:196) claimed that children's rights are more than '. . . claims of dependence . . . [they] . . . are ethical statements about the quality of a human life'. A high profile has been given to discussion about the rights of children over the past decade with many countries at least giving tacit recognition to the importance of respect for children's rights (Lansdown, 1996). Parents and members of the general community agree that in principle children have a universal right to survival and development, although whose responsibility it is and to what level such rights might be promoted and protected would be likely to cause some debate. The term 'development' refers not only to physical health, but to the 'mental, emotional, cognitive, social and cultural development' (Franklin & Hammarberg, 1995:x) in which the principle of equality is inherent. As we approach the end of a century in which understanding about the rights of children has undergone significant change, it is evident that the rhetoric generally is not translated into action, with the importance of early childhood receiving little attention in terms of its contribution to success in later life.

The moral or ethical responsibility of early childhood professionals in acting as a protector, advocate, facilitator and negotiator becomes a high priority because their intimate knowledge about individuals and extensive experience with young children place them in the best position to know what is in the best interest of the child and their family. Given that young children are vulnerable, they need special support to allow them access to their rights. Therefore, those adults who work with young children need to be aware of, sensitive to and respectful of their rights and best interests and take on an enabling role (Franklin & Hammarberg, 1995).

While the recognition of the concept of children's rights has gained greater acceptance, debate has surrounded specific definition of what such rights might be. Throughout the world, early childhood service provision has been a low priority and low status item on government agendas (Alexander, 1995). Coupled with conflicting ideologies, lack of direction and political naivety within the profession, such factors have diminished any power or credibility early childhood professionals might have had to act as advocates in promoting and protecting the rights of young children. During the 1990s, early childhood professionals in a number of countries, among them Australia, New Zealand, Canada and the United States of America, recognised the importance of developing a code of ethics or standards of practice as a means of ensuring that children's rights are identified and enhanced. Such documents provide a clear statement of goals and values that early childhood professionals can use to guide their decision making and interactions in relation to young children.

The United Nations Convention on the Rights of the Child which has been ratified by almost 200 countries (Lansdown, 1996) has provided a vehicle for those who work with young children to promote their rights. Early childhood professionals have a responsibility to become aware of its contents (Hirst, 1996) and to develop and implement policies and practice that are in line with the spirit of the Convention on the Rights of the Child. As Nutbrown (1996:101) points out, 'every educator . . . must come to realise that they . . . have a responsibility to work for children's rights and that they can do much on a day to day basis to support, extend and uphold children's rights'.

Providing quality and economically viable services

The provision of quality and economically viable services which do not compromise children's rights is another moral or ethical challenge for early childhood professionals. Recent images of parents as consumers whose purchasing power can influence the type of care and education offered within the community (Larner & Phillips, 1994) have been met with concern by many early childhood professionals. Research has revealed that parental choice of service is influenced by a range of factors (Rodd & Millikan, 1996). However, quality of service does not appear to be a high priority (Larner & Phillips, 1994). As well as offering a range of flexible services for young children and their families, pressure is also on early childhood professionals to address issues of quality assurance and improvement, the rights of the consumer and value for money in service provision (Pugh, 1996). Sometimes such issues are not incompatible with the rights and needs of young children in early care and education settings. The push towards becoming entrepreneurial and being responsive to the demands of a competitive market means that consideration of children's rights may be pushed into the background when developing new and existing services. While it is essential that early childhood services be affordable and cost efficient, these factors must be balanced against the ethical responsibility to protect children's rights. Ultimately, early childhood services cannot afford to sacrifice children's rights in order to meet short term priorities and pressures because this may in fact have long term effects on children's development as productive citizens.

There is a clear need for explicit principles and values which reflect the rights of children to high quality care and education that fosters their development and acknowledges the role of their family. Quality is not a finite goal which once attained can be checked off a list of things to do. Quality is a complex ideal which early childhood professionals continually pursue. Our understanding of quality will change over time as our understanding of young children's development, needs and rights grows. Quality in early childhood is related to high quality professional practice (Saracho, 1992) where the rights and interests of the child are regarded as the highest priority. Unfortunately, statements about goals and values and written documents such as a code of ethics are professional guidelines which can be used only to assist in decision making and conflict resolution. Such documents generally hold no legal status and those professionals whose behaviour does not conform with such guidelines are not subject to any legal or professional sanctions. Their power comes from the ethical obligation inherent in the early childhood professional's roles and responsibilities to promote and protect the rights of young children.

Many early childhood professional organisations as well as statutory bodies have put forward sets of quality indicators which can be used to assess the range of existing services. Alexander (1995:137) offered the following five central goals and values which are useful in determining to what extent children's rights come before other considerations.

- Children come first. Every child has a right to depend upon adults to provide the conditions which will enable them to reach their full potential. We all bear responsibility for all our children and it is essential that parents and carers should receive the necessary support to ensure that their children receive the best possible start in life.
- Children have a right to be recognised as people with views and interests. They have the right to be listened to and to participate in decision making about issues which affect their lives.
- Children should have the opportunity to be part of a family and community, to experience a stable learning and caring

environment which enhances their esteem as individuals, their dignity and autonomy, self confidence and enthusiasm for learning, and respect for others which ensures they are free from discrimination.

• Parents, carers and communities need to be supported in promoting the interests and welfare of their children. Children need strong adults upon whom they can depend to provide love, security and the financial resources to ensure they can access an adequate standard of living. Early years services must be rooted in local community infrastructures and provide real choice for families, particularly those on low incomes.

• Children have the right to safe play environments which provide a whole range of opportunities for autonomy, social development and recreational activity. Children and families also have the right to participate in the services provided by the retail, cultural and tourist sectors.

The services provided for children should start with and be based upon the rights and interests of the child, not from the interests of parents (although the common interests of parents and children must be recognised), nor from those of professionals, the organisation, finances, and educational fads.

Administering early childhood centres in accordance with the profession's ethical principles

One of the indicators of quality is an effective administration or management structure (Pugh, 1996). Administrative or management competence is considered to be a necessary but not sufficient aspect of leadership. Nevertheless, effective and efficient administration requires that a leader make decisions and act upon ethical principles which have been accepted and endorsed by the early childhood profession. For early childhood, administering services in an ethical manner means transforming traditional power relationships into collaborative, consultative, communicative, respectful decision making.

Effective administration or management of early childhood centres involves four major functions. These are planning, implementation, operation and evaluation (Shoemaker, 1995). Planning includes aspects of leadership, philosophy and involvement of others. Implementation includes ethical decision making and creative problem solving as well as aspects of motivation, team building and staff development. Operation refers to the knowledge base for the running of early childhood services, the choices made in relation to issues such as facilities, equipment, the use of space, room arrangement and scheduling, as well as financial management and record keeping. Evaluation refers to the ongoing learning process which provides information about the effectiveness of early childhood services and informs the management of change. Each of these four functions can involve ethical issues and dilemmas, that is, moral decision making that cannot be settled by reference to educational or developmental theory and research (Katz, 1995b) or statutory regulations. An effective leader will understand her power and status in these areas and the need to be guided by professional principles and values in order to maintain a well run centre. Where the leader understands her professional role as an administrator or manager, she will make responsible decisions which are guided by professional standards of practice and a code of ethics.

Staff selection, development and evaluation are areas which are central to the ethical administration of an early childhood centre. The quality of staff in terms of appropriate training and experience has been found to be critical for the provision of high quality services in early childhood (Bredekamp & Copple, 1997). It is important that those charged with employment of staff regard staff selection as an ethical responsibility and part of meeting the needs of young children. Shoemaker (1995:61) argues that 'The importance of providing training and development updates to all adults involved with [an early childhood centre] cannot be emphasised too highly'. She believes that the better the understanding that early childhood professionals and support staff have about what constitutes quality in early childhood services, the goals of early care and education and child development, the more responsive early childhood services can be to children and families. This is part of the ethical responsibility to provide for children's rights to quality care and education.

In addition to training opportunities, early childhood professionals need to be encouraged to regularly evaluate their performance and goals. Evaluation is an essential part of the ongoing learning process in which all professionals engage. The notion of reflective practice (Dahlberg & Asen, 1994) as a basis for evaluation of individual staff members, the organisation itself and the pursuit of quality has been endorsed by many early childhood professionals. However, evaluation is not a value-free process. Perceptions of what is important in early childhood services are based on professional and personal values. Behaviours, attitudes and attributes will be judged on the basis of such values. It is essential that leaders understand the value basis of evaluation and ensure that evaluation procedures and processes are consistent with the professional values and philosophies that guide the early childhood profession. Evaluation of staff, practice and services must be conducted within the context of social responsibility, children's rights and ethical decision making.

Where early childhood centres are administered from an ethical perspective, it is likely that positive interaction and teamwork between staff members will be evident. The creation of effective early childhood teams appears to be related to the leader's ethical decision making in relation to the employment of the best staff available and ensuring that all staff take part in regular training and evaluation. It is important that leaders make the principles and values on which they developed the administrative structure transparent for team members because this will help others understand the valid basis of administrative policies and operations.

Employing an early childhood code of ethics to guide the resolution of ethical dilemmas

Being an early childhood professional in contemporary society means more than being appropriately trained for and experienced in care and education for young children. It means adopting a particular mental set or attitude towards one's work. Members of the early childhood field increasingly regard themselves as professionals with a distinct professional identity and growing professional self esteem and confidence. Professionalism continues to be a valued goal for members of the early childhood field throughout the world. Part of being regarded as a professional is the incorporation of certain attributes into one's professional identity. Katz (1995a) describes a number of attributes which are considered to be relevant for early childhood practitioners. Among these attributes is the adoption of a code of ethics by a profession. Effective early childhood leaders will appreciate that one of the products of becoming a professional, and indeed an ethical leader, is additional moral obligations and responsibilities to children, their families, colleagues, the community and society and the profession.

The Australian Early Childhood Association (1991:3) defined its code of ethics as a 'set of statements about appropriate and expected behaviours of members of a professional working group and, as such, reflects its values'. Katz (1995b:240) considered a code of ethics to be 'a set of statements that help us deal with the temptations inherent in our occupations' which provide guidelines for deciding what is right rather than expedient, good rather than practical, and what acts may never be engaged in or condoned under any circumstances. A code of ethics can be considered to be a vehicle for protecting the rights and welfare of those who may be dependent and vulnerable as well as a means of protecting members of the profession themselves from making unsuitable decisions in relation to young children and their families. While leaders in early childhood centres might argue that they have an altruistic mission and vision and naturally would act in the best interests of young children and their families, a code of ethics provides a focus for debate about philosophy, values and ethical issues as well as being a tool for guiding the complex decision making faced in day to day work with young children and their families.

There are several reasons why early childhood professionals need a code of ethics. One reason is because they have considerable autonomy and independence over their behaviour and decisions. Decisions have to be made quickly, often without discussion with or reference to others. Such pressures may result in unsuitable behaviour or decisions which do not protect children's rights or are not in their best interests. In addition, a decision which can be rationalised and justified by reference to a code of ethics appears to carry more weight and credibility and as such is less likely to be challenged than one which does not have such a solid underpinning. A code of ethics can guide and support the leader's decision making and problem solving and give a leader greater confidence in these demanding aspects of her work.

Another reason why a code of ethics is helpful is because many situations and incidents which occur in day to day work with young children contain inherent conflict of value or interest or pose an ethical dilemma. Fleet and Clyde (1993) define ethical dilemmas as situations which involve conflict between core values and difficult, even painful choices that result in less than satisfactory outcomes. Leaders often have to take ultimate responsibility for deciding on or supporting courses of action which will affect the lives of other people. Where a decision is required but where no mutually acceptable or satisfactory options appear to exist, effective leaders will refer to the code of ethics to determine over-riding principles and values to help them work towards an optimal resolution of the dilemma.

Finally, a code of ethics is necessary because the infrastructure of the early childhood profession contains a number of features which increase the likelihood of ethical dilemmas occurring in day to day practice. These features include low status and power, a multiplicity of clients with potentially conflicting needs and interests, role ambiguity and poor integration of knowledge base and practice (Fleet & Clyde, 1993). A code of ethics can assist early childhood professionals, including leaders, to behave in ways and make decisions that do not compromise children, themselves and other parties and groups associated with early childhood centres. While a code of ethics cannot and is not intended to solve the individual and complex situations faced by early childhood professionals in their work, it does offer a tool to guide reflection, behaviour and decision making.

One of the limitations of many professional codes of ethics is that they have no power to enforce the code or apply sanctions to members who choose not to endorse or comply with or flagrantly breach the principles and values accepted by and for the professional group as a whole. Behaving in accordance with a profession's code of ethics tends to be a voluntary undertaking by individual members of that profession. For the early childhood profession, a code of ethics indicates the moral obligations and responsibilities of practitioners to individuals and groups who are associated with the field and highlights moral issues related to working with those who are vulnerable. An effective early childhood leader will act as a role model for others by using the code of ethics to explore issues which arise in practice and will work to gain acceptance of and support for ethically appropriate rules and guidelines with team members. While not asserting power over noncompliance with or breaches of the principles reflected in the code of ethics by colleagues, a leader will accept the moral responsibility for raising such issues for discussion and work towards positive resolution.

It is important for leaders to understand that a code of ethics even without sanctions can play an important role in improving the professional practice of early childhood practitioners. It can focus thinking and debate, thereby increasing understanding of and unity of purpose within the field. It can guide advocacy efforts and raise the professional standing of the early childhood field within the community. A code of ethics needs to be perceived as part of the resources available to leaders and all members of the early childhood field and as such should be central to meeting the ethical challenges faced in day to day practice.

One final area may be of interest in the discussion of the ethics of leadership. The issue of gender-specific leadership was discussed in Chapter 1. However, in the area of ethical leadership, a gender-related but not gender-specific orientation has been identified (Desjardins, 1996). It appears that men and women may use different moral orientations in their approach to leadership and the way they respond to ethical dilemmas. Desjardins (1996) argues that moral orientation has two dimensions: a justice rights orientation and a care connectedness orientation. The justice rights orientation emphasises objectivity and universality and directs the leader to treat others fairly and avoid interfering with their rights. The care connectedness orientation uses attachment and care, expressed as concern with providing for the needs of others, as guiding principles in moral decisions. Desjardins' (1996) work suggests that men appear to act more generally on the basis of the justice rights orientation with women being more frequently guided by care and connectedness values. It is important for an effective leader in early childhood, who is more likely to be a woman, to appreciate the two dimensions of moral orientation and to ensure that considerations of rights and fairness as well as attachment and care are employed when faced with ethical dilemmas and moral decision making.

In conclusion, effective leaders in early childhood appreciate their moral obligation to act with professional integrity in all aspects of their work. In exercising ethical leadership, consideration needs to be given to the clarification of personal morals and professional ethics. The effective leader will be able to clearly articulate her value system and, as a consequence, her behaviour will be perceived by others as more predictable and credible. The leader's value system should be understood by those associated with the early childhood centre to provide a rationale for the broad goals of the service, ethical decisions and choices as well as providing the basis for administrative and organisational aspects of the centre. The ethics of leadership lie in the leader's attitudes towards the involvement and participation of others in issues which affect their lives. Ethical leadership is a process of working with people to achieve specific goals which is founded on trust, values, respect, communication, collaboration and empowerment.

Epilogue

As the research which documents the link between high quality early childhood programs and children's later social and educational success accumulates, professionals who work in early childhood services will have an opportunity to articulate their vital role in facilitating young children's development and achievement. It is time for early childhood professionals to act on their own behalf and inform the public about their fundamental importance in children's development and education, their essential contribution to improving policy and decision making in care, educational and welfare areas and the cost effectiveness of their services.

To date, leadership has not been perceived as a mandatory aspect of the administrative role of the coordinator or director of an early childhood service which explains in part the continued low status ascribed to those who work in such services. However, Simons argued in 1986 that leadership could be demonstrated by early childhood practitioners if they used their skills to efficiently administer a responsive service and to initiate change in a methodical way. Since that time, the type of leadership exercised by the designated administrator of an early childhood centre has continued to be identified in research findings as one of the critical factors in the level of quality of programs provided for young children, in terms of positive results for both children and staff (Jorde-Bloom, 1997). The role of the leader and the manner in which that role is carried out has become of central importance in the provision of high-quality services (Saracho, 1992) and for determining the level of professionalism which is accorded to the early childhood field.

Jorde-Bloom (1992:138) has defined the leader of an early childhood centre as 'the gatekeeper to quality'. She argues that the role is both critical and complex, requiring conceptual and practical skill in organisational theory and leadership, child development and early childhood programming, fiscal and legal issues, and committee, parent and community relations. While high-quality services have been associated with experienced leaders (Phillips, Scarr & McCartney, 1987), other evidence reveals that training rather than work experience is the best predictor of quality early childhood services (Powell & Stremmel, 1989). However, in terms of the leadership aspect of the role, very little training has been available for those who have been employed to administer early childhood services. In Australia as in other countries, the majority of early childhood leaders have learned 'on-the-job' with support from some in-service training. As a result, the quality of leadership is unlikely to indicate the hidden and undeveloped potential of many of those in administrative positions in the early childhood field.

In order to move the early childhood field along the pathway of professionalism, access needs to be provided for practitioners to the knowledge and skills required for effective leadership in centres and in the community. The early childhood profession is dynamic and characterised by growth and change (Bredekamp & Copple, 1997). It is therefore essential that all members of the early childhood field embrace a life long learning perspective about their own development and regard leadership as a key aspect of this development. This book has addressed many of the essential issues in becoming a leader. However, the focus has been on knowledge and information. Books cannot train people! The next step is for the reader to put some of the ideas into practice and to begin to integrate the theory with professional practice. Support for the development of these nascent skills can be obtained from in-service courses and from undertaking further study in courses which provides a focus on leadership in the early childhood context. Leaders in early childhood will be required to demonstrate an orientation and commitment to further professional training and development to be able to be responsive to change.

The recent introduction of quality assurance mechanisms such as voluntary accreditation of early childhood services as a means of setting minimum national standards will produce further changes in the role of the leader. One of the basic premises of accreditation is that leadership is related to quality programs (National Association for the Education of Young Children, 1984). The leader is likely to be responsible for ensuring a nurturing and educational environment for children, as well as fulfilling the responsibility for the recruitment, training and development of staff, the support and development of parents, and establishing and personifying the 'public face' of the centre and the early childhood profession in contacts with other professionals and the general community. It will be a challenge for leaders to meet these new demands in a style that communicates a confident professionalism. The opportunity for community acknowledgement of a new level of professionalism in early childhood hinges on the development of the leadership abilities of members of the early childhood field.

References

Adair, J. 1986, *Effective Teambuilding*, Gower Pub. Co., Aldershot

Adler, A. 1958, *What Life Should Mean To You*, Capricorn Books, G.P. Putnam's Sons, New York

Albert, L. and Einstein, E. 1986, *Strengthening Stepfamilies*, American Guidance Service, Minnesota

Alberti, R.E. and Emmons, M.I. 1970, *Your Perfect Right: A Guide to Assertive Behaviour*, Impact, San Luis Obispo

Alexander, G. 1995 'Children's rights in their early years. From plaiting fog to knitting treacle', *The Handbook of Children's Rights: Comparative Policy and Practice*, eds B. Franklin and T. Hammarberg, Routledge, London

Allen, K.K. and Miller, M.S. 1990, 'Teacher-researcher collaboratives: Cooperative professional development', *Theory into Practice,* vol. 24, no. 3, pp. 196–202

Almy, M. 1975, *The Early Childhood Educator at Work*, McGraw-Hill, New York

——1985, 'New challenges for teacher education: Facing political and economic realities', *Young Children*, vol. 40, no. 6, pp. 10–11

——1988, 'The early childhood educator revisited', *Professionalism and the Early Childhood Practitioner*, eds B. Spodek, O. Saracho & D. Peters, Teachers College Press, New York

Anastasiow, N. 1988, 'Should parent education be compulsory?', *Topics in Early Childhood Special Education*, vol. 8, no. 1, pp. 60–72

Australian Early Childhood Association Inc. 1991, 'Australian Early Childhood Association Code of Ethics', *Australian Journal of Early Childhood,* vol. 16, no. 1, pp. 3–6

Bailey, R. 1986, *Coping with Stress in Caring,* Blackwell Scientific Publishing, Oxford

Barbour, N. 1992, 'Meeting the child care needs of the 1990s', *Child and Youth Care Forum,* vol. 21, no. 5, pp. 297–8

Benton, D. and Halloran, J. 1991, *Applied Human Relations, An Organisational Approach,* 4th edn, Prentice-Hall, Englewood Cliffs

Berk, L.E. 1997, *Child Development,* 4th edn, Allyn and Bacon, Needham Heights

Biber, B. 1988, 'The challenge of professionalism: Integrating theory and practice', *Professionalism and the Early Childhood Practitioner,* eds B. Spodek, O. Saracho & D. Peters, Teachers College Press, New York

Block, P. 1981, *Flawless Consulting: A Guide To Getting Your Expertise Used,* Learning Concepts, Austin

Bogue, E.G. 1985, *The Enemies of Leadership: Lessons for Leaders in Education,* Phi Delta Kappa Educational Foundation, Bloomington

Bolton, R. 1986, *People Skills: How to Assert Yourself, Listen to Others and Resolve Conflicts,* Prentice-Hall, Sydney

Borgia, E.T. and Schuler, D. 1996 'Action research in early childhood education', *ERIC Digest,* EDO-PS-96-11, ERIC Clearinghouse on Elementary and Early Childhood Education, Illinois

Bredekamp, S. 1992, 'Composing a profession', *Young Children,* vol. 47, no. 2, pp. 52–4

Bredekamp, S. and Copple, C. 1997, *Developmentally Appropriate Practice in Early Childhood Programs,* rev. edn, National Association for the Education of Young Children, Washington DC

Brill, N.I. 1995, *Working With People,* 5th edn, Longman, New York

Brunner, C. 1994, 'Emancipatory research: Support for women's access to power', paper presented at the *1994 Annual Conference of the American Educational Research Association,* New Orleans

Burton, F.R. 1986, 'Research currents: A teacher's conception of the action research process', *Language Arts,* vol. 63, pp. 718–23

Caldwell, B. 1984, 'Advocacy is everybody's business', *Child Care Information Exchange,* vol. 54, pp. 29–32

——1984, 'Growth and development', *Young Children,* vol. 39, no. 6, pp. 53–6

Carlisle, H.M. 1979, *Management Essentials: Concepts and Applications,* Science Research Associates Inc., Chicago

Carnall, C. 1990, *Managing Change,* Routledge, London

——1995, *Managing Change in Organisations,* 2nd edn, Prentice-Hall, Hemel Hempstead

Caruso, J.J. 1991, 'Supervisors in early childhood programs: An emerging profile', *Young Children,* vol. 46, no. 6, pp. 20–6

Cherniss, C. 1995, *Beyond Burnout: Helping Teachers, Nurses, Therapists and Lawyers Recover from Stress and Disillusionment,* Routledge, London

Children's Services Centres Regulations 1988, Victorian Government Printer, Melbourne

Clift, R., Veal, M., Johnson, M. and Holland, P. 1990, 'Restructuring teacher education through collaborative action research', *Journal of Teacher Education*, vol. 41, no. 2, pp. 52–62

Clyde, M. 1989, 'Editorial Comment', *Australian Journal of Early Childhood*, vol. 14, no. 1, p. 2

Clyde, M. and Rodd, J. 1989, 'Professional ethics: There's more to it than meets the eye', *Early Child Development and Care*, vol. 53, pp. 1–12

——1992, 'Child minders or professional child care worker? Perceptions of family day care providers', *Early Child Development and Care*, vol. 81, pp. 55–63

——1993, 'A comparison of Australian and American centre-based caregivers' perceptions of their roles', *Advances in Early Education and Day Care*, ed. S. Reifel, JAI Press, Greenwich

Coady, M. 1991, 'Ethics, laws and codes', *Australian Journal of Early Childhood*, vol. 16, no. 1, pp. 17–20

Cohen, A.C. 1988, *Early Education: The Parent's Role*, Chapman Publishing, London

Cohen, L. and Manion, L. 1994, *Research Methods in Education*, 4th edn, Routledge, London

Cox, E. 1996, *Leading Women: Tactics for Making the Difference*, Random House, Sydney

Curran, D. 1989, *Working With Parents: A Guide to Successful Parent Groups*, American Guidance Service, Minnesota

Curry, M. 1989, 'Early childhood advocacy. Evolving into an advocate, a personal case', *Dimensions*, vol. 18, no. 1, pp. 23–4

Dahlberg, G. and Asen, G. 1994, 'Evaluation and regulation: A question of empowerment', *Valuing Quality in Early Childhood Services: New Approaches to Defining Quality*, eds P. Moss and A. Pence, Paul Chapman Publishing, London

Daughtrey, A.S. and Ricks, B.R. 1994, *Contemporary Supervision*, 2nd edn, McGraw-Hill, Singapore

Davis, H. 1985, 'Developing the role of parent advisor in child health services', *Partnership Paper 3*, eds E. De'Ath & G. Pugh, National Children's Bureau, London

Desjardins, C. (1996) 'Gender based teambuilding: Strengths men and women bring to leadership roles', proceedings of *Annual International Conference The Olympics of Leadership: Overcoming Obstacles, Balancing Skills, Taking Risks*, National Community College Chair Academy, Phoenix

Dreikurs, R. and Soltz, V. 1982, *Happy Children: A Challenge to Parents*, 8th edn, William Collins Sons & Company, Glasgow

Drucker, P. 1973, *Management*, Harper & Row, New York

Dunphy, D. 1986, *Organisational Change By Choice*, Prentice-Hall, Sydney

Ebbeck, M. 1990, 'Preparing early childhood personnel to be pro-active, policy making professionals', *Early Child Development and Care*, vol. 58, pp. 87–95

Elliot, J. 1991, *Action Research for Educational Change*, Open University Press, Buckingham

Ellison, C. and Barbour, N. 1992, 'Changing child care systems through collaborative efforts: Challenges for the 1990s', *Child and Youth Care Forum*, vol. 21, no. 5, pp. 299–316

Feeney, S., Christensen, D. and Moravcik, E. 1996, *Who Am I in the Lives of Children? An Introduction to Teaching Young Children*, 5th edn, Charles Merrill Publishing, Columbus

Feeney, S. and Kipnis, K. 1991, 'Professional ethics in early childhood education', *Australian Journal of Early Childhood*, vol. 16, no. 1, pp. 40–2

Finkelstein, B. 1988, 'The revolt against selflessness: Women and the dilemmas of professionalism in early childhood education', *Professionalism and the Early Childhood Practitioner*, eds B. Spodek, O. Saracho & D. Peters, Teachers College Press, New York

Fleer, M. and Waniganayake, M. 1994, 'The education and development of early childhood professionals in Australia', *Australian Journal of Early Childhood*, vol. 19, no. 3, pp. 3–13

Fleet, A. and Clyde, M. 1993, *What's In a Day: Working in Early Childhood*, Social Science Press, Wentworth Falls

Franklin, B. and Hammarberg, T. 1995, *The Handbook of Children's Rights: Comparative Policy and Practice,* Routledge, London

Galen, H. 1991, 'Increasing parental involvement in elementary school: The nitty-gritty of one successful program', *Young Children*, January, pp. 18–22

Galinsky, E. 1981, *Between Generations: The Six Stages of Parenthood*, Times Books, New York

——1986, 'What really constitutes quality care?', *Child Care Information Exchange*, vol. 51, pp. 41–7

——1990, 'Why are some parent/teacher partnerships clouded with difficulties?', *Young Children*, July, pp. 2–3 and pp. 38–39

George, C. and Cole, K. 1992, *Supervision in Action*, 3rd edn, Prentice-Hall, Sydney

Getskow, V. 1996, 'Women in community college leadership roles', *ERIC Digest*, ERIC Document, ED400025, ERIC Clearinghouse on Elementary and Early Childhood Education, Illinois

Gibbs, C.J. 1990, 'Student teacher opinions on educational issues—an initial survey, 1989', *Australian Journal of Early Childhood*, vol. 15, no. 2, pp. 38–42

Glass, G.V. 1987, 'What works: Politics and research', *Educational Researcher*, vol. 16, no. 3, pp. 5–10

Goffin, S.G. 1988, 'Putting our advocacy efforts into a new context', *Young Children*, vol. 43, no. 3, pp. 52–6

Goffin, S.G. and Lombardi, J. 1988, *Speaking Out: Early Childhood Advocacy*, National Association for the Education of Young Children, Washington

REFERENCES

Goodnow, J. 1989, 'Setting priorities for research on group care for children', *Australian Journal of Early Childhood*, vol. 14, no. 1, pp. 4–10

Goodnow, J. and Collins, W.A. 1990, *Development According To Parents: The Nature, Sources and Consequences of Parents' Ideas*, Hove Erlbaum, Hillsdale

Grant, L. 1997, '50 most powerful women in Britain. Part 2. The age of optimism', *The Guardian*, May 27, pp. 2–4.

Greenberg, P. 1989, 'Parents as partners in young children's development and education: A new curriculum fad? Why does it matter?', *Young Children*, vol. 44, no. 4, pp. 61–75

Gupton, S.L. and Glick, G.A. 1996, *Highly Successful Women Administrators: The Inside Stories of How They Got There*, Corwin Press, Thousand Oaks

Hall, V. 1996, *Dancing on the Ceiling: A Study of Women Managers in Education,* Paul Chapman Publishing, London

Hamner, T.J. and Turner, P.H. 1996, *Parenting in a Contemporary Society*, 3rd edn, Allyn and Bacon, Needham Heights

Hampton, D.R., Summer, C.E. and Webber, R.A. 1983, 'Group decision making is not always better', *Organisational Behavior. Concepts, Controversies and Applications*, ed. S. Robbins, Prentice-Hall, Englewood Cliffs

Harrison, J. 1991, *Understanding Children: Towards Responsive Relationships*, Australian Council for Educational Research, Melbourne

Harvey, T.R. 1990, *Checklist for Change. A Pragmatic Approach to Creating and Controlling Change*, Allyn and Bacon, Needham Heights

Hasenfeld, Y. 1983, *Human Service Organizations*, Prentice-Hall, Englewood Cliffs

——1992, *Human Services as Complex Organisations*, Prentice-Hall, Englewood Cliffs

Hayden, J. 1996, *Management of Early Childhood Services: An Australian Perspective*, Social Science Press, Sydney

Henderson, A. 1987, *The Evidence Continues to Grow: Parent Involvement Improves Student Achievement*, National Committee for Citizens in Education, Columbia

Hennessy, E., Martin, S., Moss, P. and Melhuish, E. 1992, *Children and Day Care, Lessons From Research*, Chapman Publishing, London

Hennig, M. and Jardim, A. 1976, *The Managerial Woman*, Pocket Books, New York

Henry, M. 1996, *Young Children, Parents and Professionals Enhancing the Links in Early Childhood*, Routledge, London

Hersey, P. and Blanchard, K. 1988, *Organisational Behaviour*, Prentice-Hall, Englewood Cliffs

Hess, R.D. 1980, 'Experts and amateurs: Some unintended consequences of parent education', *Parenting in a Multicultural Society*, eds M. Fantini and R. Cardenas, Longman, New York

Hirst, K. 1996, 'Parents and early childhood educators working together for children's rights', *Respectful Educators—Capable Learners: Children's Rights and Early Education*, ed. C. Nutbrown, Paul Chapman Publishing, London

Hodgkinson, C. 1991, *Educational Leadership: The Moral Art*, State University of New York Press, Albany

Honig, A.S. 1996, 'Early childhood education: Training for the future', *Early Childhood Development and Care*, vol. 121, pp. 135–45

Hopkins, D. 1990, *A Teacher's Guide To Classroom Research*, Open University Press, Philadelphia

Hord, S.M. 1986, 'A synthesis of research on organisational collaboration', *Educational Leadership*, vol. 43, no. 5, pp. 22–6

Hostetler, L. 1991, 'Collaborating on behalf of young children', *Young Children*, vol. 46, no. 2, pp. 2–3

Johnson, D.W. 1996, *Reaching Out: Interpersonal Effectiveness and Self-Actualisation*, 6th edn, Prentice-Hall, Englewood Cliffs

Johnson, D.W. and Johnson F.P. 1996, *Joining Together: Group Theory and Process*, 6th edn, Prentice-Hall, Englewood Cliffs

Jones, C.C. 1980, *Leadership and the Use of Power in ECE Administration*, Early Childhood Education Administration Institute, Rockville

Jorde-Bloom, P. 1982, *Avoiding Burnout: Strategies for Managing Time, Space and People in Early Childhood Education*, Gryphon House, Mt Rainier

——1992, 'The child care centre director: A critical component of program quality', *Educational Horizons*, Spring, pp. 138–45

——1995, 'Shared decision making: The centre piece of participatory management', *Young Children*, vol. 50, no. 4, pp. 55–60

——1997, 'Leadership: Defining the elusive', *Leadership Quest*, vol. 1, no. 1, pp. 12–15

Jorde-Bloom, P. and Sheerer, M. 1991, *The Head Start Leadership Training Program*, National-Louis University, Evanston

——1992, 'The effects of leadership training on child care program quality', *Early Childhood Research Quarterly*, vol. 7, pp. 579–94

Jorde-Bloom, P., Sheerer, M. and Britz, J. 1991, 'Leadership style assessment tool', *Child Care Information Exchange*, vol. 87, pp. 2–15

Kagan, S.L. 1988, 'Dealing with our ambivalence about advocacy', *Child Care Information Exchange*, vol. 51, pp. 31–4

——1994, 'Leadership: Rethinking it—Making it happen', *Young Children*, vol. 49, no. 5, pp. 50–4

Karpin, D. 1995, *Enterprising Nation: Renewing Australia's Managers to Meet the Challenges of the Asia Pacific Century*, Australian Government Printing Service, Canberra

Katz, L. 1977, *Talks With Teachers*, National Association for the Education of Young Children, Washington DC

——1988, 'Where is early childhood as a profession?', *Professionalism and the Early Childhood Practitioner*, eds B. Spodek, O. Saracho & D. Peters, Teachers College Press, New York

——1995a, 'The nature of professions: Where is early childhood education', *Talks With Teachers: A Collection*, L. Katz, Ablex Publishing Corporation, Norwood

——1995b, 'Ethical issues in working with young children', *Talks With Teachers: A Collection*, L. Katz, Ablex Publishing Corporation, Norwood

Kelly, V. 1996, 'Action research and the early years of education', *Early Years*, vol. 17, no. 1, pp. 41–6

Kemmis, S. and McTaggert, R. 1988, *The Action Research Planner*, Deakin University Press, Waurn Ponds

Kinney, J. 1992, 'New thoughts on child care administration and leadership involving emerging information on the psychology of women', paper presented at the *1992 Conference of the National Association for the Education of Young Children*, New Orleans

Kolb, D.A. 1984, *Experience as the Source of Learning and Development*, Prentice-Hall, Englewood Cliffs

Kolb, D.M. 1989, 'Supervisory techniques for positive performance', *Day Care and Early Education*, Fall, pp. 16–19

Kostelnik, M.J. 1984, 'Real consensus or group think?', *Child Care Information Exchange*, August, pp. 25–8

Kotzman, A. 1989, *Listen To Me, Listen To You*, Penguin, Ringwood, Victoria

Kurtz, R.R. 1991, 'Stabilizer, catalyst, troublemaker or visionary—which are you?', *Child Care Information Exchange*, vol. 77, pp. 27–31

Lansdown, G. 1996, 'Respecting the right of children to be heard', *Contemporary Issues in the Early Years: Working Collaboratively for Children*, 2nd edn, G. Pugh, Paul Chapman Publishing, London

Larner, M. and Phillips, D. 1994, 'Defining and valuing quality as parents', *Valuing Quality in Early Childhood Services: New Approaches to Defining Quality*, eds P. Moss and A. Pence, Paul Chapman Publishing, London

Lay-Dopyera, M. and Lay-Dopyera, J.E. 1985, 'Administrative leadership styles, competencies and repertoires', *Topics in Early Childhood Special Education Administration*, vol. 5, no. 1, pp. 15–23

Levine, M. 1992, 'Observations on the early childhood profession', *Young Children*, vol. 47, no. 2, pp. 50–1

Lewin, K. 1974, 'Frontiers in group dynamics: Concept, method and reality of social sciences: Social equilibria and social change', *Human Relations*, June, pp. 5–14

Lewis, G., Schiller, W. and Duffie, J. 1992, 'Calling the tune or dancing to it: Early childhood teacher education in Australia', *Early Child Development and Care*, vol. 78, pp. 57–76

Lieberman, M. 1956, *Education as a Profession*, Prentice-Hall, Englewood Cliffs

Likert, R. 1961, *New Patterns of Management*, McGraw-Hill, New York

McLennan, R. 1989, *Managing Organisational Change*, Prentice-Hall, Sydney

McNaughton, G. 1996, 'Researching for quality: A case for action research in early childhood services', *Australian Journal of Early Childhood*, vol. 21, no. 2, pp. 29–33

Marsh, C. 1995, 'Quality relationships and quality practice in the nursery school', *International Journal of Early Years*, vol. 3, no. 2, pp. 29–39

Maslow, A. 1970, *Motivation and Personality*, Harper & Row, New York

Mason, E.J. and Bramble, W.J. 1989, *Understanding and Conducting Research: Applications in Education and the Behavioural Sciences*, 2nd edn, McGraw-Hill, New York

Maxcy, S.J. 1991, *Educational Leadership: A Critical Pragmatic Perspective*, Bergin and Garvey, New York

Mitchell, A. 1989, 'Kindergarten programs that are good for children and parents', *Principal*, vol. 68, no. 5, pp. 17–19

Morgan, G. 1997, 'What is leadership? Walking around a definition', The Center for Career Development in Early Care and Education, Wheelock College, Boston

Mulligan, V. 1996, *Children's Play: An Introduction for Care Providers*, Addison-Wesley Publishers, Canada

National Association for the Education of Young Children, 1984, *Accreditation Criteria and Procedures of the National Academy of Early Childhood Programs,* National Association for the Education of Young Children, Washington DC

Neugebauer, R. 1983, 'Do you have delegation phobia?', *Child Care Information Exchange*, March/April

——1984a, 'Who's responsible for making your team work?', *Child Care Information Exchange*, January, pp. 4–6

——1984b, 'Step by step to team building', *Child Care Information Exchange*, June, pp. 9–13

——1985, 'Are you an effective leader?', *Child Care Information Exchange*, vol. 46, pp. 18–26

Neugeboren, B. 1985, *Organization, Policy and Practice in Human Services*, Longmans, New York

Nutbrown, C. 1996, *Respectful Educators—Capable Learners: Children's Rights and Early Education*, Paul Chapman Publishing, London

Page, J.M. 1995, *Another World Like Here: Future Studies and Early Childhood Education*, Masters Thesis, University of Melbourne, Melbourne

Pascal, C. 1992, 'Advocacy, quality and the education of the young child', *Early Years*, vol. 13, no. 1, pp. 5–11

Perreault, J. 1991, 'Society as extended family: Giving a childhood to every child', *Dimensions*, vol. 19, no. 4, pp. 3–8

Peters, D.L. 1988a, 'Current issues and future needs in staff training', paper presented at the *National Policy Conference on Early Childhood Issues*, Washington DC

——1988b, 'The child development associate credential and the educationally disenfranchised', *Professionalism and the Early Childhood Practitioner,* eds B. Spodek, O. Saracho & D. Peters, Teachers College Press, New York

Phillips, D., Scarr, S. and McCartney, K. 1987, 'Child care quality and children's social development', *Developmental Psychology*, vol. 23, pp. 537–43

Piaget, F. 1986, 'Piaget's theory of director development', *Child Care Information Exchange*, vol. 50, pp. 10–13

Porter, H. 1997, '50 most powerful women in Britain. Part 1. Smashing the glass ceiling', *The Guardian*, May 26, pp. 2–4.

Posner, B.Z and Brodsky, P. 1994, 'Leadership practices of effective student leaders: Gender makes no difference', *National Association of Student Personnel Administrators Journal*, vol. 31, no. 2, pp. 113–20

Powell, D.R. 1989, *Families and Early Childhood Programs*, National Association for the Education of Young Children, Washington DC

Powell, D.R. and Stremmel, A.J. 1987, 'Managing relations with parents: Research notes on the teacher's role', *Continuity and Discontinuity of Experience in Child Care*, eds D.L. Peters & S. Kontos, Ablex, Norwood

——1989, 'The relation of early childhood training and experience to the professional development of child care workers', *Early Childhood Research Quarterly*, vol. 4, pp. 339–56

Pugh, G. 1996, *Contemporary Issues in the Early Years: Working Collaboratively for Children*, 2nd edn, Paul Chapman Publishing, London

Rayner, M. 1995, 'Children's rights in Australia', *The Handbook of Children's Rights: Comparative Policy and Practice,* eds B. Franklin and T. Hammarberg, Routledge, London

Rennie, J. 1996, 'Working with parents', *Contemporary Issues in the Early Years: Working Collaboratively for Children*, 2nd edn, ed. G. Pugh, Paul Chapman Publishing, London

Report of the Review of Early Childhood Services 1983, *Future Directions For Children's Services in Victoria*, Government Printing Service, Melbourne

Ripley, D. 1994, 'Vision, values and virtues: A principal's curriculum for a good school', *Canadian School Executive*, vol. 13, no. 7, pp. 16–20

Robbins, S. 1996, *Organizational Behavior, Concepts, Controversies and Applications*, 7th edn, Prentice-Hall, Englewood Cliffs

——1980, *The Administrative Process*, 2nd edn, Prentice-Hall, Englewood Cliffs

Rodd, J. 1987, 'It's not just talking: The role of interpersonal skills training for early childhood educators', *Early Child Development and Care*, vol. 29, no. 2, pp. 241–52

——1988, 'What's in a name? Changing the image of early childhood professionals', *Australian Journal of Early Childhood*, vol. 13, no. 3, pp. 47–8

——1989, 'Better communication = better relationships', *Day Care and Early Education*, vol. 17, no. 1, pp. 28–9

——1990, 'Keeping up with the latest: How about an early childhood clearing house?', *Australian Journal of Early Childhood*, vol. 15, no. 2, pp. 26–9

——1992, 'Child care coordinators' understanding of teamwork in early childhood services', unpublished research, School of Early Childhood Studies, University of Melbourne, Melbourne

——1996, 'Towards a typology of leadership for the early childhood professional of the 21st century', *Early Child Development and Care*, vol. 120, pp. 119–26

——1997a, 'Learning to develop as early childhood professionals', *Australian Journal of Early Childhood*, vol. 22, no. 1, pp. 1–5

——1997b, 'Learning to develop as leaders: Perceptions of early childhood professionals about leadership roles and responsibilities', *Early Years*, vol. 18, no. 1, pp. 40–6

Rodd, J. and Clyde, M. 1991, 'A code of ethics: Who needs it?', *Australian Journal of Early Childhood*, vol. 16, no. 1, pp. 24–34

Rodd, J. and Millikan, J. 1996, 'Parental perceptions of early childhood services for pre-primary children in Australia', *Early Child Development and Care*, vol. 101, pp. 89–100

Rogers, C. 1961, *On Becoming a Person*, Houghton Mifflin, Boston

Ryan, P. 1989, 'Leaving the industry: A report on staff turnover in New South Wales long day care centres', *Rattler*, vol. 9, pp. 4–5

Saracho, O.N. 1988, 'Cognitive style and early childhood practice', *Professionalism and the Early Childhood Practitioner*, eds B. Spodek, O. Saracho & D. Peters, Teachers College Press, New York

——1992, 'The future of teacher education in the changing world', *Early Child Development and Care*, vol. 78, pp. 225–29

Schein, E.H. 1980, *Organizational Psychology*, 3rd edn, Prentice-Hall, Englewood Cliffs

Schaffer, H.R. 1990 *Making Decisions About Children: Psychological Questions and Answers*, Basil Blackwell Ltd, Oxford

——1996, *Social Development,* Basil Blackwell Ltd, Oxford

Schiller, J. 1987, 'Peer supervision: Learning more about what we do', *Australian Journal of Early Childhood*, vol. 12, no. 3, pp. 43–6

Schiller, P.B. and Dyke, P. 1990, *Managing Quality Child Care Centres: A Comprehensive Manual for Administrators*, Teachers College Press, New York

Schoonover, S.C. and Dalziel, M.M. 1986, 'Developing leadership for change', *Management Review*, July, pp. 55–60

Schrag, L., Nelson, E. and Siminowsky, T. 1985, 'Helping employees cope with change', *Child Care Information Exchange*, September, pp. 3–6

Selye, H. 1975, *Stress Without Distress*, Lippincott, Philadelphia

Sergiovanni, T.J. 1990, *Value-Added Leadership: How To Get Extraordinary Performance in Schools*, Harcourt, Brace, Jovanovich Publishing, Florida

Shimoni, R. 1991, 'Professionalisation and parent involvement in early childhood education: Complementary or conflicting strategies?', *International Journal of Early Childhood*, vol. 23, no. 1, pp. 11–20

REFERENCES

Shoemaker, C.J. 1995, *Administration and Management of Programs for Young Children,* Prentice-Hall, Englewood Cliffs

Sigston, A. 1996, 'Research and practice—worlds apart?', *Psychology in Practice With Young People, Families and Schools,* eds A. Sigston, P. Curran, A. Labram and S. Wolfendale, Fulton Publishers, London

Silin, J.G. 1988, 'Becoming knowledgeable professionals', *Professionalism and the Early Childhood Practitioner,* eds B. Spodek, O. Saracho & D. Peters, Teachers College Press, New York

Simons, J. 1986, *Administering Early Childhood Services,* Southwood Press, Sydney

Simpson, D.T. 1977, 'Handling group and organisational conflict', *The 1977 Annual Handbook for Group Facilitators,* eds J.E. Jones & J.W. Pfeiffer, University Associates Inc, La Jolla, California

Spodek, B. 1987, 'Thought processes underlying preschool teachers' classroom decisions', *Early Child Development and Care,* vol. 28, pp. 197–208

——1988, 'Implicit theories of early childhood teachers: Foundations for professional behavior', *Professionalism and the Early Childhood Practitioner,* eds B. Spodek, O. Saracho & D. Peters, Teachers College Press, New York

Spodek, B., Saracho, O. and Peters, D. 1988, *Professionalism and the Early Childhood Practitioner,* Teachers College Press, New York

Stonehouse, A. and Creaser, B. 1991, 'A code of ethics for the Australian early childhood profession: Background and overview', *Australian Journal of Early Childhood,* vol. 16, no. 1, pp. 7–16

Stonehouse, A. and Woodrow, C. 1992, 'Professional issues: A perspective on their place in pre-service education for early childhood', *Early Child Development and Care,* vol. 78, pp. 207–23

Storm, S. 1985, *The Human Side of Child Care Administration: A How To Manual,* National Association for the Education of Young Children, Washington DC

Sull, T. 1997, 'Of critical consideration: Teachers' beliefs and the mentoring relationship', *Leadership Quest,* vol. 1, no. 1, pp. 7–9

Takanishi, R. 1986, 'Early childhood education and research: The changing relationship', *Theory into Practice,* vol. 20, no. 2, pp. 86–92

Tayler, C. 1992, 'Early childhood teacher education in Australia', *Early Child Development and Care,* vol. 76, pp. 3–25

Teacher Education: Directions and Strategies, 1990, Ministry of Education, Youth and Women's Affairs, New South Wales

Thorner, L. 1997, 'What is leadership? Definition # 4001', *Leadership Quest,* vol. 1, no. 1, pp. 4–5

Tripp, J. 1990, 'The role of research', *Children and Society,* vol. 4, no. 1, pp. 120–5

Vander Ven, K. 1988, 'Pathways to professional effectiveness for early childhood educators', *Professionalism and the Early Childhood*

Practitioner, eds B. Spodek, O. Saracho & D. Peters, Teachers College Press, New York

——1991, 'The relationship between notions of care giving held by early childhood practitioners and stages of career development', *Early Childhood Towards the 21st Century: A Worldwide Perspective*, ed. B. Po-King Chan, Yew Chung Education Publishing, Hong Kong

Varner, A.F. 1984, 'Risk taker, caretaker or undertaker: which are you?', *Child Care Information Exchange*, August, pp. 1–3

Wadsworth, Y. 1997, *Do It Yourself Social Research*, 2nd edn, Allen & Unwin, Sydney

Walker, E. H. 1995, *Teamwork in Child Care: A Study of Communication Issues in Forming a Team*, Masters Thesis, University of Adelaide, Adelaide

Wallace, J. and Wildy, H. 1995, 'The changing world of school leadership: Working in a professional organisation today', *Practising Administrator*, vol. 17, no. 1, pp. 14–17

Waniganayake, M. 1997, 'Leadership in early childhood in Australia: A national review', paper presented at the *Research Symposium on the International Leadership Project*, University of Oulu, Oulu, Finland, May

Watts, B. and Patterson, P. 1984, *In Search of Quality. Home and Day Care Centre: Complementary Environments for the Growing Child*, Lady Gowrie Child Care Centre, Brisbane

Webb, R. 1996, 'Changing primary classroom practice through teacher research', *Education 3 to 13*, vol. 24, no. 3, pp. 18–26

Whitebrook, M. and Bellm, D. 1996, 'Mentoring for early childhood teachers and providers: Building upon and extending tradition', *Young Children*, vol. 52, no. 1, pp. 59–64

Whitford, B.L., Schlechty, P.C. and Shelor, L.G. 1987, 'Sustaining action research through collaboration: Inquiries for invention', *Peabody Journal of Education*, vol. 64, no. 3, pp. 151–69

Wilkins, A. and Blank, H. 1986, 'Child care: Strategies to move the issue forward', *Young Children*, vol. 42, no. 1, pp. 68–72

Wofford, J. 1979, ' "Know thyself"—The key to improving your leadership style', *Child Care Information Exchange*, November

Wolfendale, S. 1983, *Parental Participation in Children's Development and Education*, Gordon and Breach, New York

——1986, 'Involving parents in behaviour management: A whole school approach', *Support for Learning*, vol. 1, no. 4, pp. 32–8

——1996, 'Enhancing the effectiveness of parents: Applications of psychology', *Psychology in Practice With Young People, Families and Schools*, eds A. Sigston, P. Curran, A. Labram and S. Wolfendale, Fulton Publishers, London

Woodcock, M. 1979, *Team Development Manual*, Halsted Press, New York

Woodcock, M. and Francis, D. 1981, *Organisational Development Through Teambuilding*, Gower Publishing, Aldershot

REFERENCES

Yonemura, M. 1986, *A Teacher at Work: Professional Development and the Early Childhood Educator*, Teachers College Press, New York

Zaltman, G., Duncan, R. and Holbek, J. 1973, *Innovation and Organization*, Wiley, New York

Index